My Father's Last Meatballs

A Heavenly Entrée

PAULA MAIDA MOONEY

MAIDAVALE PRESS

This book is dedicated to my loving family, and especially my husband, Richard. Although he sometimes gave me *acido* (ah-chee-doa) when I was writing this memoir, I knew that his actions came from love. Richard took me on many trips, but none more meaningful than this spiritual journey to Italy.

♥

TO THE READER

THIS STORY YOU ARE ABOUT TO READ is about the men in my life; more significantly, first and foremost, the first male that many females will ever encounter—the relationship between a daughter and her father. Along the way, it deftly mixes an Italian immigrant family, the Second World War, Brooklyn in the 1940s and 1950s, the inevitable moves to the suburbs, and a batch of relatives who grew up and grow old together. Finally, it pays tribute to an enduring parental relationship and the extraordinary journey I took to Italy, where a chance encounter spiritually realigned my perception of life and death.

I have written this story in the third person point of view, which some readers may find inappropriate for a memoir. But I did so because it was easier for me to detach myself and write—family members became characters in a book (including myself). Because this time of my life was so intensely painful and frightening, it was difficult to move-on; symptoms of post-traumatic stress disorder started to appear. Writing in this manner became a catharsis and eventually in my emotional healing. (Please note: these are my opinions and perceptions as they actually transpired.)

As I have since learned from the readings of Gary Zukav and other proponents of spiritual growth and development, "There is no time between a daughter's loving intention toward her father and the soul of her father understanding that intention."

I sincerely hope that my fellow Baby Boomers read my story, especially if you are dealing with aging and sick parents. Two things I have learned from my experience is that "growing older is not to be feared," and "a little miracle can come into your life when you least expect it." When it happens, accept it with love and gratitude.

With heartfelt thanks and affection,

Paula

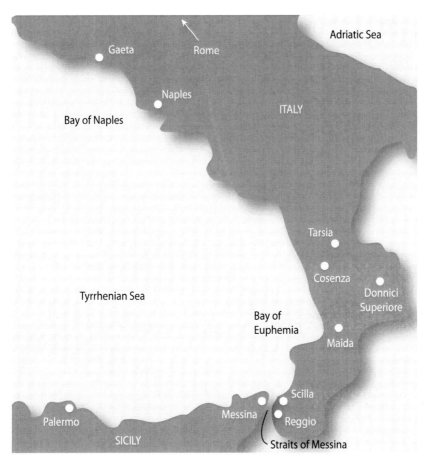

The Journey—from Sicily to Southern Italy

CONTENTS

♥

PROLOGUE

Januᴀʀʏ 17ᴛʜ ɪs ᴀ ᴅᴀʏ that remains carved in my brain
as sharply as an epitaph on a stone. It is the day my father,
"My Johnny," died.

That winter in New York seemed as though the snow
would never stop falling and none of us would ever feel warm
again. It was the coldest winter reported in 25 years. I stood
there, feeling the numbness I felt all the time these days,
looking out of my 28th floor window.

It seems like a joke, really. Here I was, in the Sutton
Place apartment my father was proud as punch of my having ("You should see Paula's apartment, what a spread!" he
would beam, managing to delight, embarrass, and please me
all at the same time). I looked around the room I'd decorated
so pleasingly. Everything about it suggested quiet comfort.
I'd learned that from my mother. My eyes fell upon the soft
pink of the walls, the blue and cream Schumacher stripe silk
curtains, and the overstuffed down and feather velvet sofa.
Odd, how none of this could coax any comfort back now.

I gazed transfixed at the majestic lights on the 59th
Street Bridge. Ice caps on the East River were flowing

downstream. All I could think about was "My Johnny." He was everything to me: the reason I always wanted to be the best I could be, the person I'd go to for advice about a job I was considering, or for his blessing on my marriage to Richard. I could hear him now—"He's a helluva nice guy, Paula. Believe me, I have my concerns, but if you love him, I'll be there for you."

When was he ever not there for me? "Oh Daddy," I uttered, the tears starting again. How could I not think about the love he showered on me for every one of my years, the joy and the laughter he brought into my life? How lucky I was to have this man as my father, and how angry I had become.

In less than three months I had lost both my parents to lung cancer. My mother died the previous October 17th. One week after her funeral, my father was diagnosed with the same disease. Impossible, it seemed, but all too true. Exactly three months to the day, he was gone.

Family members were quick to tie the uncanny timing together. "Rose wanted Johnny with her," they would tell me, as though I would be okay thinking my Mom and Dad were together again after he'd spent his last ten years taking care of her.

I personally thought it was more an act of retribution than love. My memories of the two of them came round and round like carousel horses, each with a different countenance: all those years of Mom's declining health; Dad's plans to go to Italy for the first time as it became clear that my mother's illness was terminal; stories of how they met and when I was born; their wartime secrets: the joy they would always tell me about having me; and, all the photos they took. "Wasn't Paula beautiful?" "Did you ever see such big brown eyes?" "Oh look, that's her on her second birthday." I was adored, unconditionally and completely. How do you replace that? Little did I know that on that bitter winter day, my spiritual journey was about to unfold.

This is how this love story begins—a boy meets a girl . . .

Chapter 1

ON A BUS TO
RED BANK

NEW YORK CITY—John Maida was twenty-three years old and working in the beverage industry that hot, summer day when fate stepped in and introduced him to the girl he would marry. Arriving at the terminal in ample time to catch his Greyhound bus to Red Bank, New Jersey, he was eagerly looking forward to the day's excursion. His job required him to call on a liquor store at the Jersey Shore, and he was happy to be leaving the sweltering streets of the city.

The temperature would be above ninety again, making this the fifth day in a row of hot, sticky weather. In a few hours he would be miles away from the crowded pavement he walked daily, and if time allowed, he could grab a swim and take a walk on the beach. While waiting for the bus to arrive, he noticed an attractive girl on the platform. She was wearing a pair of white, crocheted gloves. He knew exactly how they were made, because his mother liked to crochet.

Fortunately for him, they both boarded the same bus. He waited for her to select a seat. As she walked to the rear of the bus, he admired her derriere, smiled, and quickly jumped at the opportunity to sit next to her. An impressive-looking girl with thick, auburn hair that fell in gentle waves to her shoulders, she was well built. Not too skinny, he thought. He wasn't attracted to thin girls—he preferred a little meat on the bone. At first, he hesitated to talk to her, as she had an air of quiet elegance that left him uncertain on how he should proceed. He watched her graceful movements as she put her small tote on the rack above the seat. How crisp and unsoiled her white eyelet cotton dress was, even down to her shoes—clean, white pump heels to match her ensemble. But most of all, he admired her auburn hair. When the light fell upon it, it seemed to glisten, like the color of bronze. In spite of the heat wave, she looked comfortable and refreshed. She even smelled clean, a hint of lavender water, he suspected. He watched her with interest, as her long, tapered fingers proceeded to open the book, and she started to read it: *Gone with the Wind*. His eyes caught the title of the book, but he was not sure he had heard of it. This young woman looked like no girl he had dated in Brooklyn.

As a child, John had poor eyesight, but he could see very clearly now, and he wanted to know more about this luscious creature sitting next to him. Like any young man, it took him a while to decide how to start a conversation. Finally, he smiled at her and said, "Hello." She looked up from her book with inquisitive, light brown eyes to see the young man sitting next to her. He continued, "Excuse me. I don't mean to be forward, but I was admiring you and the book you're reading."

"Have you read it?" she asked in a gentle tone . . . not a hint of Brooklynese.

"No," he said. "But any book that big looks pretty impressive." She smiled, ready to return to her reading. "My name is John Maida. I live in Brooklyn with my folks, and I'm going to work in Red Bank today. What's your name?"

"Rose," she said. "Rose Emilia Marasco."

"I *knew* you were Italian," he said, smiling broadly. "That beautiful hair could only be Italian."

By the time he got off the bus in Red Bank two hours later, John knew quite a bit about this pretty girl. He whistled as he walked to his appointment, with her phone number securely in his pocket, wondering if she was thinking of him on the remainder of her ride. She'd said she was going to Cape May to visit with her Aunt Mary and Uncle Ralph.

Aunts and uncles were for her what moms and dads were for other people, he'd come to find out. He took out the paper on which she'd written her telephone number and address, 184 Waverly Place. That's in Greenwich Village, he supposed. He didn't even care that she was three years older than he; it was no big deal. But he couldn't help shake the feeling that their families were worlds apart. Heck, they were both Italian; how bad could they be?

"I was raised by my Aunt Mamie, my mother's sister," she said, adding, "And my mother's four brothers." He shook his head at the conversation. All adults, with no brothers and sisters around—it was hard for him to fathom.

"Oh, I have brothers, three of them."

" You weren't raised in the same home?" John couldn't help but ask.

She carefully chose her words and added, "After the twins were born, another brother soon followed." Her parents, Emilia Delli Paoli and Anthony Marasco, resided in New

York City and Chappaqua, New York. Were they prominent or society types, he wondered?

Nope, he wouldn't have liked growing up in such a household with all adults. He was happy to be one of eight children. Imagine, giving their first kid away. Mama could never on her life do that—what's the matter with those people? He felt anger and dismay. How could parents do that to a little girl? It wasn't the first time he would find her family unlikable. He'd come right out and asked her, "Why did they allow you to be raised by your aunt and uncles?"

She instinctively hunched her shoulders toward her ears as though to say, "Damned if I know . . ." Instead she said, "Well, my uncles are prominent attorneys. My mother and aunt really look up to them. They treat their brothers like gods, and maybe they thought they were doing me a favor to be around people like this." Her words didn't ring true. She knew it.

And John knew it. "*Marrone*," he said to himself, "parents who give their kid away."

He could see her family was as different from his as night and day—Brooklyn and Manhattan. She'd mentioned that her maternal grandfather was a banker with offices on Broome Street in New York City. The grandfather had come from Salerno, Italy, but he might as well have come from Mars, as far as John was concerned.

As Rose continued her ride on the bus that day, she thought of how comfortable she felt talking to that sweet fellow. He was so open and friendly that he instantly put her at ease. She wasn't used to people like that. In her household, people were decidedly more proper and formal. She felt that familiar sadness creep into her mind. The fact that her parents parceled her out to be raised by an aunt was an issue that would always haunt and depress her. Oh, she knew her aunt and uncles loved her, but it wasn't the same.

Emilia Delli Paoli Marasco was a stately, patrician looking woman with a lofty attitude. Her physical stature and comely looks would have made her a fine subject for the portrait artist John Singer Sargent. Rose was both impressed and intimidated by her mother—the only thing they had in common was the color of their hair. A formidable woman, she always found fault with her daughter and constantly criticized Rose.

"Can't you stand up straighter?" "Your brothers are younger than you, but even they're better behaved." "What's wrong with you, Rose?"

John couldn't wait to get home to call her! They had their first date five days later. He naturally suggested a Saturday or any evening after six o'clock, and was surprised when she said she didn't work, so it didn't matter to her. Oh right, then it came back to him. On the bus she'd said she wanted to be a nurse. But her uncles refused to send her to nursing school. Heaven forbid she had to take care of diseased people. They thought the job too subservient a profession for their only niece. All three of her brothers had attended college and pursued their interests. But she was strictly forbidden to follow her pursuits. It never occurred to John that her loneliness, her sense of being the odd person out, was a key reason their relationship took off so quickly. Someone finally wanted her and cared about her.

"Do you like the movies?" John asked. She had to think about it for a moment. She wasn't used to being asked her opinion—about anything. But here was this lovely fellow who seemed to want to know everything about her. "Do you like lasagna? My mother makes the best lasagna. Do you sew?

My sisters all sew. My sister Catherine—we're very close, her and me—she can't wait to meet you." John couldn't wait to introduce Rose to a real family!

John was the second son in the pecking order. And he was acutely aware that his father was a good provider for his family. Although they were Italian immigrants, John knew his family was more fortunate than others. His father, Giuseppe, was eighteen years old when he arrived in New York City from the port of Naples in 1902. Six years later he met and married Angelina Capalbo, who had migrated to America when she was sixteen. With no fanfare and no money, Giuseppe (twenty-four) and Angelina (eighteen) set about making this new country their home and building a life together, and apparently very much together. Between 1909 and 1927, Angelina bore him four sons and four daughters. Giuseppe took particular pride in this even division, as though providing the mathematical precision of God. "Grazie Dio!" escaped from his lips as surely as, "Angelina, *quando mangiamo*?" (Angelina, when do we eat?)

Giuseppe never touched hard liquor, but wine was different—a gift from the soil. He would recall his fond memories in the hills of Cosenza, a province of Calabria, where grapes and olives were so much a part of his life. Kissed by the sun, the grape was sacred. Even the Catholic Church knew this and used wine for sacramental purposes. And Giuseppe knew something about the art of winemaking. In another coincidence of timing, a childhood friend from Cosenza was now in America making wine for a living. The Bisceglia Brothers operated a large cannery business and produced wines from their California vineyards.

Soon Giuseppe was recruited by the brothers to work as a foreman in their plant in New York. He was just what they needed: a friend from the old soil, as trustworthy as a saint, with a working knowledge of winemaking (like the era itself, far simpler than today's gussied-up term, oenologist). For thirteen years during Prohibition, Giuseppe was making a hefty sum of money—particularly, because in those years when you made a dollar, you kept a dollar. No income tax had yet come knocking on any doors.

With his relative affluence, Giuseppe was able to buy a three-family brick townhouse in Brooklyn. He was proud that his daughters could wear nice clothing. Angelina loved her little fox head fling and dangly earrings, cameos, and ropes of beads and pearls around her zaftig 5'3" frame. She adorned her heavyset body in ways that pleased both her and her husband. For her part, Angelina cooked, entertained friends, and cared for the eight children diligently and unceasingly. Of all the siblings, John felt closest to his sister Catherine and brother Ernest. And close was inescapable, given their sheer numbers and proximity. The living quarters were on two floors: three bedrooms and one bathroom upstairs, and downstairs in the basement a second bathroom, big kitchen, and a large, separate dining room.

The kids often slept three or four to a bed. No one had any privacy, and no one was ever lonely. Sharing the daily chores, eating meals together, and the Sunday ritual of attending Mass together united the family. No one ever dared to complain—Giuseppe knew to be firm with the children when needed, but he knew how to be a loving father even more. Angelina was devoted to him and was subservient to his wishes. Why, if it were not for him, she would not have six of her siblings living in Brooklyn. He paid for their passage from Naples to New York, one by one. Only one sister remained in Tarsia to care for their aging parents.

The Maida household was a flurry of excitement the day John was bringing Rose home for a Sunday family dinner. This was the first girl he'd brought home outside of the neighborhood, so everyone was curious about whom they'd be meeting. He told them all about her background and how lousy it was that her parents sent her away, to a chorus of commiseration. His parents thought maybe her parents were too poor to raise her. "No, Mama, no, Papa. They just wanted to raise their sons without her around."

"It can't be. I never heard of such a thing . . . ." Giuseppe uttered in Italian.

None of them knew quite what to expect when Rose showed up, escorted by the proud beau that he was that day, their son Johnny. They greeted her warmly, taking her hat and coat. The sisters fondly caressed the soft wool of the cashmere coat, and then checked the label inside the seam of her hat. Elbowing each other, each sister wanted to be near Johnny's new girl.

"Ahma so 'appy my son Johnny bringa nice-agail-a home." With that, Angelina left them to talk with Johnny's new girlfriend while she went to finish the cooking.

Mary, the eldest daughter, quickly jumped up. "Wait, Mama, I'll help you in the kitchen," she said, and excused herself.

Rose instantaneously felt the warmth and love of the Maida household. It seemed to be everything hers was not: slightly chaotic, everybody talking at once, and the sisters wanting to know more about her, starting with her dress.

"What a beautiful shade of blue," Catherine commented. "Did you get that at Ohrbach's?" Catherine wasn't sure there was any nicer store, so that's the one that popped into her mind. An air of joviality filled the house and every moment of the visit. The meal went on for hours, with one dish more delicious than the next and everyone taking credit for something.

"Oh, you like that? Teresa made it."

"I made the sausage and peppers," Anna piped in.

"And what did the boys do?" Rose asked while looking at the brothers clustered in a row.

Ernie smiled broadly. "We made sure they did it right," he grinned, tongue planted firmly in cheek.

"Bruno brought the bread," yelled the youngest sibling, Joseph Jr. The constant chatter, the laughs, and, when they were all saying their good-nights, the hugs they showered upon her—she felt happier than perhaps she could ever remember. At last she had finally experienced, up close and personal, a closely knit family.

Chapter 2

A SECRET
WEDDING

AFTER SIX MONTHS OF A COURTSHIP that she
discreetly withheld from her family, Rose finally
decided that it was time to introduce John at a family gathering. Within moments it was clear that John Maida was no
match for the Marasco-Delli Paoli clan. An uncomfortable
visit ended with their offering limp or no handshakes to a
shaken Johnny. John left with sweaty palms, dejected, head
down, and shoulders narrowed. The minute he'd gone, they
let Rose know in no uncertain terms that he was completely
unacceptable.

The uncles, as well as her parents, all stood firm. "You're
going out with a man beneath your status," they said harshly,
decreeing, "please don't bring him here again." They even
found his olive complexion too dark for their liking. "Are
you sure he isn't Sicilian?" they sarcastically chided.

Rose felt a private war raging within her as surely as the
war that had erupted in Europe. Here it was with World War
II stalking fear upon them all. She felt as though her heart

were breaking while the world seemed to be tearing itself apart. John's younger brother, Ernie, had already enlisted in the navy. That winter, John asked his sister Catherine to buy a new dress. "What for?" she wanted to know.

"For something important to me, Katy," he said.

Catherine approached her father for some money. "Dad, Johnny is taking me out with some friends and I need a new dress." Giuseppe didn't question it. In fact, he offered to go with her. "It's okay, Pa, Johnny will come with me." What she hadn't expected was that Rose would be there, too. "What the heck," she figured, the more, the merrier. Catherine bought a forest green suit with a hat that matched. Both Johnny and his girlfriend said it would be perfect for the occasion. "What occasion?" she asked, unsuspectingly. Little did she know that she was going to Johnny's wedding.

The young couple was anxious to get married, but realizing the objections of the bride's family, they secretly planned a small wedding. John asked his best friend, Frank (nicknamed Italo), to be his best man. Rose asked her high school girl friend Jeanette to act as her maid of honor. On Thanksgiving weekend, John and Rose were wed at St. Francis Xavier Church on West 16th Street in Manhattan. Catherine, John's younger sister, was the only family member present.

When Catherine realized what was happening, she was shocked, fearfully asking her brother, "But what, are you crazy? Why didn't you tell Mama and Papa you were getting married? Oh Johnny, this will kill them . . . my God, they weren't invited to their own son's wedding." John's emotions were a crazy mix of elation and trepidation on this, his wedding day. He hated marrying without his parents there.

Rose had said bitterly at the time, "They gave me away as a little girl, and now, when I ask them to do this for me, they refuse because they don't think John is worthy of me." Sparks would have been flying, so the decision was made not to include any parents.

Johnny explained this to Catherine, saying with finality, "Let me be happy, Katy. We just couldn't do this any other way." Before they left on their weekend honeymoon to the Catskills, John and Rose broke the news to both sets of parents by telephone. The Marasco-Delli Paoli clan raged and the Maidas wept. Being devout Catholics, and sorrowful though it was, the deed was done. John and Rose were married in the eyes of God.

Chapter 3

THE WAR YEARS

E MOTIONS WERE RUNNING HIGH IN BOTH FAMILIES. When they attempted a dinner together in Brooklyn, each family was visibly uncomfortable with the other. The Marascos wore elegantly tailored suits and expensive silk dresses. The Maidas, true to their roots, wore freshly starched and ironed clothes. Giuseppe wore his usual vest with his omnipresent watch fob looped from pocket to button. The girls and Angelina donned their Sunday best, which proved to be no match for the finery that adorned the Marasco-Delli Paoli women.

It wasn't just appearances, either. They had nothing to say to each other. "Well, we're family now," Giuseppe said, as they all sat down to a dinner Angelina and her daughters had spent days preparing. He carefully raised his glass of wine. *"Salut, a nostro figlio y nuova figlia"* (to our son and new daughter).

The Marasco-Delli Paolis looked stricken. He was not their son. And how dare these immigrants refer to Rose as their new daughter! They claimed they didn't understand

Italian. Johnny and Rose exchanged rolled-eye looks of resignation and did their valiant best to get through dinner.

The scene was a microcosm of the angry factions everywhere in the world. In 1939, war had erupted between Germany and the Allies. When Germany joined forces with Italy, Giuseppe was devastated along with the thousands of Italian immigrants who were now proud to call themselves American citizens. Early on, war had seemed remote, taking place "over there." Then America entered the war after "a day of infamy," as Franklin Delano Roosevelt called the day when Japan attacked the United States at Pearl Harbor.

The newlywed couple was hardly alone in feeling worried and overwhelmed by the times in which they found themselves. By now, they were living in a small three-room walk-up apartment on West 15th Street. Two of his brothers had already been sent to fight overseas. "Oh, Johnny," Rose lamented. "What will I do if you have to go, too?" Her question, echoing in household after household across the country, was answered with her worst fears being realized.

Shortly thereafter, a letter arrived from Headquarters, Southern N.Y. Recruiting & Induction District on Lexington Avenue, New York, that ordered John Maida to report for duty in the United States Army. About two weeks shy of his twenty-fifth birthday, at 5 foot 10 inches, 155 pounds, and with weak eyesight, he didn't share Rose's dim view of his being drafted. He was eager to serve his country. He felt proud that he was being called to do his part. How could he sit on the sidelines when he wanted to fight for his country?

"I'm not gonna let a pair of glasses stand between me and this damned war," he resolved. "Besides," he figured, "Uncle Sam could use me in plenty of other ways." For one thing, he was a good salesman, and a pretty good typist. And, like so many unstoppable young men and women, he was determined to do his part. The government needed no convincing. He landed a position in the Post Exchange and army administration as a clerk typist in support of the U.S. Army Air Corps making their daily bombing raids on Germany and readying the troops for the D-Day invasion.

Although Private First Class John Maida was never sent to the front lines, he was stationed in England for more than three years. He witnessed the devastation that occurred during the air raids with bombs dropping over London as buildings, homes, and lives were being destroyed. He ran for shelter along with everyone else and lifted bodies from beneath the rubble. People had to pull together or perish. Fright was not the reigning emotion; defiance and anger were! He was helping the English in any way he could.

While John was stationed in England, Rose asked him to contact a friend of hers, Elizabeth. For many years in high school, these women were pen pals. A warm correspondence grew between them, and Rose was eager for Johnny to meet her. As fate would have it, he was able to locate Elizabeth. And it proved a fortuitous friendship for this American and English woman to have a personal ally in these times. Not particularly pretty, she was terribly nice with a sassy sense of humor. They were young people living in a war zone. John was happy to provide Elizabeth with rations he could get from the army's PX. Her eyes invariably lit up when he'd arrive with canned goods, chocolate, or cigarettes. In turn, Elizabeth proved a delightful friend whose accent never ceased to delight him, and whose flat, which she shared with two roommates, gave him some brief hours of haven from his army quarters.

Since there was no Fed Ex, no e-mail, and no transatlantic calls then, getting and sending mail became all the more meaningful in those years. John was glad his job at the PX helped him make sure soldiers got their letters and packages from home. He and Rose wrote frequently, but it was often several weeks before regular mail would actually reach them, though military V-Mail arrived faster, in its censored and limited format.

For her part, Rose had decided that there was nothing to do but make the best of her circumstances. She didn't dare dwell on the uneasy emotion that she'd been abandoned again. John had encouraged her to keep busy and to make sure she took good care of herself. He got her laughing about what a celebration they'd have when he returned. "Have you any idea how many raviolis and cannolis are gonna be coming out of Mama's kitchen?" he wrote on the back of his picture. Rose stayed close to that picture, and to the other photos of them in their apartment. She wasn't alone, she assured herself.

It was dawning on Rose that she liked her newly found independence. She listened to the news on the radio and read the *New York Journal American* every day; she instinctively knew that she had to take part in supporting this cause. The country needed all the able bodies it could get in the line of defense. Like millions of other women, she would find a job. Women had gone to work in droves to replace the men who'd joined the armed forces. From 1940 to 1945, the number of women working increased by 50 percent. "Rosie the Riveter" was the pumped-up and pretty symbol invented by public relations and embraced by the public. "We can do it!" read the Rosie posters. And Rose Maida decided, yes, she could do it too.

Taking her place among the hard-working women in factories across the country, Rose found a job in Manhattan's
garment district, sewing uniforms. Going to work every day
gratified her and indulged her need to feel wanted. And she
especially enjoyed the camaraderie of the other women. Eating lunch together, sharing stories about their husbands and
boyfriends overseas, and discussing the weddings they'd had
gave her a sense of empowerment. For the first time she felt
she was in control of her own life. Her family was appalled.

"A factory! For God's sake, Rose Emilia, we didn't raise
you to be a seamstress!" her Uncle Frank bellowed.

She held her own. "It's a good job, and it's where I'm
needed right now. I'm appreciated . . . and, if you'll excuse
me, I'm going home." She was completely comfortable taking
buses or trains and inviting a friend or two over for a cup of
coffee, as it increasingly dawned on her that she was living
under her own roof and no one else's.

Even so, being separated by thousands of miles, particularly at the tender start of a marriage, is hardly the founda-
tion upon which relationships are built. As with so many
couples, this was a time that tested their spirit and commitment to each other. It created stress and marital strain,
though in those days no one dared talk about being unhappy
or depressed, particularly in Italian families. "Don't let on,"
was the unspoken maxim. And if it was articulated, it was
usually accompanied by, "Nobody has to know your business." Keeping up appearances was all-important.

Neither John nor Rose let on if anything was bothering them, or if the distance was driving a wedge between
them. This was war! How dare they let their own personal
happiness become an issue! The world at large set the stage
for lives and decisions everywhere. On May 8, 1945, Prime

Minister Winston Churchill announced that the Germans had surrendered and the war was over. Huge crowds gathered outside Buckingham Palace, cheering and waiting for King George VI and Queen Elizabeth and their daughters Princesses Elizabeth and Margaret to make their victory appearance on the balcony.

In America, President Harry Truman, who was celebrating his sixty-first birthday that day, dedicated the victory to Franklin D. Roosevelt, his revered predecessor who had died less than a month before. As his death had filled hearts with enormous sadness, so the end of the war caused an eruption of joy and celebration unlike most people had ever felt or seen. The allied world was jubilant! Thousands of people took to the streets, kissing, hugging, and cheering. Pubs were running dry. The war was finally over. Sons, husbands, and fathers would be returning home. John and his two brothers would be reunited with their families once again and their lives would resume in Brooklyn.

Chapter 4

THE BOYS
COME HOME

I<small>T'S BEEN SAID</small> that America's greatest generation was the dedicated group of servicemen and women who fought in World War II. It isn't that other wars have not been waged with staggering courage, but perhaps that the sides of good and evil, right and wrong, seemed so clearly drawn then. All Americans were making great and small sacrifices everywhere. Loved ones remain memorialized in yellowing photographs that were kept on mantels and shelves. The soundtracks being played were of the big bands—Tommy Dorsey, Guy Lombardo, and Glenn Miller, with the likes of Frank Sinatra, Bing Crosby, and Perry Como crooning.

Soldiers were returning home bursting with dreams, longing to be back with their families and friends. With his meritorious decorations and citations, John came home to an America filled with patriotism. They had gone above and beyond any call of duty, exhibiting inordinate valor and a palpable love of country. Many thousands among them were the sons the immigrants gave to America. With sentiments of victory and pride running high, with women having gone to work in factories, assembly lines, and aircraft facilities to do their part, these soldiers came home to a different America from the one they left.

John received his honorable discharge from the army a year after the war ended. After three years away from his bride and family, he came home twenty pounds heavier, more muscular, and with a more attractive face. In fact, he now bore a close resemblance to the actor Fred MacMurray. Friends and family would comment, "Look what the Army did for you—you came back and look like a Hollywood star!"

Laughing it off, he would say, "You mean Fred MacMurray looks like me!" John's skin was darker, more olive, and his hair was wavier, except he kept it cut so close to his head that it was hard to discern the curl. Both men had the same open, you'd-be-inclined-to-like-him face. The lower half of their faces looked like carbon copies. Even their voice qualities were similar. But he wasn't an actor. He was a soldier who made it home, and he was now unemployed. Returning GIs were entitled to participate in the Servicemen's Readjustment Act, better known as the GI Bill of Rights. It offered assistance in housing, business, and education and one-year unemployment compensation, the fifty-two/twenty clause that gave the unemployed veteran twenty dollars a week for fifty-two weeks. While many servicemen accepted mortgage and education assistance, Italian families had developed a proud work ethic that excluded handouts like unemployment compensation and welfare payments. So it was that many returning servicemen entered the public sector with police, postal, railways, and federal or state employee jobs with their benefits.

All four Maida sons had made it safely through the war and were back home again. The house in Brooklyn was once again filled with laughter, music, and hearty appetites. The kitchen soup line, quickly reinstated by Angelina, was now feeding four sons and four daughters, all with spouses. Many of them ended up living in the same neighborhood: one of them living in an apartment in the same house; one next door; one down the street. It wasn't an uncommon scene but rather an instinctive re-creation of an Italian village, with the butchers, bakers, fish markets, and grocery stands all within walking distance.

Life would now return to normal, and the boys could pursue their American Dream to become successful, own a home, and raise bambinos. A boom was on—economic, social, and familial. A new generation was being born, soon to become known as the Baby Boomers.

Chapter 5

A PRIVATE
HOMECOMING

AGAINST THE VAST BACKDROP OF MILLIONS of servicemen returning, jobs being filled, and women taking care of their homes and husbands, couples were nonetheless struggling with readjustments. For his part, John had seen the destruction of war up close while bunking with soldiers, being with the English during the air raids, and enduring part of their triumphs and pains. He had grown up. Rose had changed, as well. They were not the same people they'd been five years earlier.

Rose wasn't quite sure what day her husband would be arriving home. She had struggled with confusing, conflicting emotions, elated at his homecoming but far less sure of what it meant for her. She had quit her job with reluctance and annoyance with herself. "I should be happy!" she said. "Johnny'll be home any day!" She would never say aloud what she was feeling, but she'd become a happier person having a job and living on her own. She wondered if she'd stay this happy.

"Stop that!" she silently reprimanded herself. "Of course I'll be happy—it will be wonderful building our life together again!" She was determined to make it happen, too. Always a fastidious and clean person, the apartment sparkled by the week she expected her husband back. She'd bought a new dress and went out of her way to make sure her hair and the little make-up she wore would be the way he liked it. Every day she wondered if today would be the day. Then, on a Wednesday morning, the bell rang, followed by a two-at-a-time scampering up the stairs and a knock on the door. "Rose! Rose! I'm home!"

Her heart started beating wildly as she opened the door. The moment that followed had that time-stood-still quality; a husband and wife, yet two strangers in many ways, stood ready to welcome each other into their arms. She watched him break into a huge, Cheshire cat smile. He stepped forward and swept her up in an encircling, never-let-you-go hug, literally lifting her off her feet, as all thoughts of concern vanished from her mind. She started crying, then laughing, then crying. "Johnny! Johnny! Sweetheart! I'm so happy you're home, look at you, you're so handsome."

They covered their faces with kisses, both of them crying now. He stood back, holding her arms between his hands. "Lemme look at you. *Mangia!* You are one beautiful woman, but you're thinner." They kissed, kissed, kissed—their lips, cheeks, foreheads—it must've been a hundred times. And he hadn't even fully come into the apartment yet. Finally, he stepped inside, holding Rose's hand. "Look at our wonderful home, Rose. My God, how I've missed being here, being with you."

"Johnny," she asked automatically, "you hungry? What can I make you? I have pasta *piselli* in the refrigerator. I have a meatloaf ready to put in the oven." She'd cooked a lot in the previous days, knowing sooner or later, he'd be here. He didn't answer right away. He seemed mesmerized, taking in every detail of the small apartment—the photos lined up on the oak bookcase, his family's pictures, her stern-looking family peeking out from behind a silver frame they'd given them for their wedding, the yellow gingham curtains she'd hung in the kitchen, and the red Formica kitchen table gleaming in the sunshine.

Then he was in the bedroom, and he turned and saw her blush. "I don't know about you," he said, "but I'd like to start our reunion here."

Chapter 6

MOVING TO BROOKLYN

THE PHRASE, "THE RABBIT DIED" is the way it was described then. In the 1940s, a rabbit test is how women were checked for pregnancy. Their urine was injected into a rabbit. The little creature would have an ovarian reaction—which, barbaric though it sounds now—required an autopsy to diagnose. If its ovaries proved enlarged, then a woman was indeed pregnant.

Rose didn't know how to announce her pregnancy to Johnny. She herself was simultaneously pleased, frightened, and oddly comforted. "Imagine, a baby!" twirled round and round in her mind. Once again, the same relief she'd felt at marrying came over her. I belong, she thought. I have my own family now. Oh, there were plenty of attendant worries, but she couldn't let them cloud her focus. Johnny was home for good. They were having a baby. She decided to make one his favorite meals; linguine with fresh clams to start, followed by veal piccata with zucchini.

At five o'clock sharp, she heard his footsteps nearing the door and his familiar, like-clockwork, "Angel, I'm home." She always met him at the door with a hug and a little kiss. Tonight was no exception. "Hmmm," he said immediately. "Somethin' smells good on that stove."

"It's your favorite," she said, smiling broadly.

"Lemme wash my hands, I'll be ready in a second." He emerged, eager to have dinner. "Oh, Angel, this is great . . ." he said, chewing his first forkful of linguine. Rose ate sparingly, not unusual for her these days, but she still enjoyed her sweets. Her satisfaction was watching him down his food with gusto. They talked about his day, a local parade in the neighborhood, and their impending move. Johnny had broached the subject a few weeks back that moving to Brooklyn to be near the family would be good for both of them—versus "living all by ourselves in the city." She actually liked the idea. That large, loving family had quickly made her feel as though she'd always been surrounded by bunches of brothers, sisters, *goomaras*, *goomparas*.

As she poured their espresso, she said, "Johnny, I have some good news . . ." He was reaching for a biscotti in front of him on the table as she continued, "I'm pregnant."

His hand paused in mid-air. He looked up at her and a full three seconds elapsed, as though he needed to fully absorb what he'd just heard, before he stood up, broke out into the biggest smile, exclaiming, "No! Yeah? Really?" "Really?" he repeated two or three times.

She said, laughing, "Really! Really!"

He put down the biscotti that just moments ago was his focus, stood up and knelt down beside Rose. "You'll be a wonderful mother. I love you. I love this baby. . . ." His eyes filled with tears, as did Rose's.

Then, as though a better idea struck him, he took both her hands in his and stood up so that she had to stand, as well. Extending his arms, he put his cheek close to hers and began dancing with her as he sang, "Lemme call you sweetheart . . . I'm in love with you . . ."

And so Rose and Johnny and baby-to-be settled into a two-room basement apartment right next door to his parents. The ensuing months were a contented time for the both of them. Rose settled in to her newfound place, not only as a member of the family but as an expectant mother, and John was adjusting to civilian life once again.

Bay Ridge, Brooklyn, was row after row of neatly kept, small, multiunit brownstones with tiny gardens in front. Women wore hats and gloves to church and housedresses at home, and kids were found on roller skates or bikes or playing ball in the cement driveways that separated the red rectangular brick buildings. The avenues were dotted with storefronts with apartments above them, where the merchants' families often lived. A subway ride cost a nickel.

The families living cheek by jowl were Italian, Jewish, Irish, and Scandinavian immigrants, a true ethnic diversity. Neighbors knew each other well. People walked to do their shopping, to take their kids to school, and to pick them up. Men delivered milk and ice for the icebox, which was how foods were kept refrigerated. Rotary phones were the only kind available, as was the party line phone service. Television had yet to enter the home, and radio was king. You could hear its sound in every apartment at some hour of every day, from Italian operas to baseball games. Walter Winchell's show mixed entertainment and national news with each story delivered in a rapid-fire staccato style and punctuated with the urgent tapping of a telegraph key; "Good evening,

Mr. and Mrs. America and all the ships at sea," was his invariable greeting.

It was a time when people were civil to each other: "Good morning, Mrs. Maida, Good morning, Mr. Weiss." The streets were safe, doors often went unlocked, and it was an easy commute by subway to New York City, where John now worked for the United States Postal Service.

Every morning around five o'clock a.m., John would get up and within half an hour be on the BMT subway to the General Post Office Building at 33rd Street and Eighth Avenue.

He thought it was the most beautiful building in the city. It was massive and it took up two city blocks, made of stone with imposing classical columns. Etched into its frieze was inscribed, "Neither snow, nor rain, nor heat, nor gloom of night stays these couriers from the swift completion of their appointed rounds." He took these words to heart. Day after day he would sort mail, stuff it into his large, tan leather carrier bag, and then deliver it. If anything, his job was keeping him in good physical condition, and for this he was grateful. The idea of going to a gym to work out was unheard of at that time.

While John was at work, Rose would spend her days with her extended family. Meeting with her sister-in-laws over coffee and conversations, or watching Angelina prepare supper in her well-stocked kitchen, she never felt bored. She especially delighted in watching Angelina's short, thick fingers roll out hand-made noodles, prepare a variety of tomato sauces, mix chopped meat and seasonings for meatballs, or stuff fresh artichokes until they brimmed with freshly grated breadcrumbs, garlic, and Parmigiana cheese. She watched, learned, and developed her own thoughts on the culinary arts.

As Rose's belly was getting larger, she voraciously read cookbooks and home decorating magazines. When Johnny came home, she made sure dinner wound be on the table by five-thirty p.m. and no later. Having been up so early, and working such a long and strenuous day, she knew he would be famished. John hated to admit it, but he was beginning to think that Rose was a more versatile and better cook than his mom. She seemed to experiment more with food, coming up with different dishes that he had never eaten before.

Entertaining was something they did frequently as a couple. John would invite friends and family over for dinner, so he could show off his wife's new culinary skills. Even Ben and Haddie Schaffer, John's partner at work and his wife, would exalt over Rose's brisket and potato pancakes. "Rose," Ben would tease, "are you sure you're not Jewish?"

Rose's pregnancy was uneventful enough. In those days, when contractions started, husbands dutifully brought their wives to the hospital—often with a brother or sister accompanying them, checking the woman in, and then returning home until a nurse called to deliver the news of the birth. The closest a man might come to wanting to be near his wife would be to wait it out in the waiting room. If that's what he did, the room would fill, hour after hour, with additional family members.

That year, Rose read a novel in which the beautiful and independent heroine was named Paula. She liked the sound of the name, although some family members had suggested Patricia with a birth proximate to St. Patrick's Day. However, Paula it was! With an olive complexion, almond-shaped brown eyes, and a little mop of wavy, dark hair, an infant daughter was born to John.

Paula was unconditionally adored, the object of kisses and cooing from dozens of family members, but none prouder or more heartfelt than her father. All fathers think their baby daughters are beautiful. But John felt for sure that he had a real beauty; the nurses in the maternity ward seemed to confirm his thinking.

The following five years were nothing extraordinary, except for the birth of more cousins for John's little girl. By the time Paula could speak, she referred to her father as "My Johnny." Rose knew she was up against a formidable partnership.

For it had begun—the first time a father holds his infant daughter, the way he looks into her eyes, and the tender hold of her little fingers grasping his. The feeling is mutual—he is her first love and her hero.

The birth of the baby into the family made life much easier for Rose and John; finally some civility ensued amongst the in-laws. During the summer months, Rose's Aunt Mamie and her mother would rent a summer cottage in Seaside Park on the Jersey Shore. As its name suggests, it was an enclave of oceanfront cottages with nothing but fresh air, sand, and the Atlantic Ocean to enjoy all day. For a kid, it was nirvana. The two elderly women cooked and cleaned while Rose took care of her daughter.

On Friday nights, John drove down from Brooklyn, and they would have a late-night supper discussing what had transpired during the week. John eagerly looked forward to spending time with his little girl. The routine was always the same for father and daughter, with mornings crabbing together on the pier, then grabbing a swim, and taking an afternoon nap. After dinner, which the matriarch ladies cooked to perfection, Rose, John, and their little girl would take a walk on the boardwalk. John would show Paula how to play Skee-Ball while the scent of freshly made caramel popcorn enticed them all. Warm summer nights at the Jersey Shore, catching lighting bugs, and having her father put her to sleep with an imaginative story bonded their relationship for life. He was her Johnny, just hers!

After much insistence on John's part, Rose gave birth to her second daughter, Marian, so named after the Catholic Church decreed the "Marian Year." With another beautiful girl, whose looks rivaled their first born, John was ecstatic.

Paula was instantly jealous of all the attention her new sister was attracting. But after the initial excitement wore off and the years passed, Paula happily realized that her baby sister was Mommy's girl. No need to worry, she still had her Johnny under her spell. And the several-year age difference gave her an edge. That same year that John's second daughter was born also marked the passing of his beloved father. Neighbors stopped over every day and evening to see what they could do for the family, never empty-handed, bringing food, fresh-baked bread, or a bottle of wine. It was a painful passing for a sweet, gentle man. Giuseppe died of colon cancer.

Angelina and the children heard him scream for days in agony. *"Lassa lai eeda!"* "Let it stop!" His adult children tended him throughout, while Angelina dutifully changed his colostomy bag, with the foul odor filling the room, which they would then try to camouflage by scouring floors and walls with strong-scented bleaches. It was a horrible time for

John and would leave an indelible mark on him. To see how this disease ravaged his beloved father's body and mind was a memory he tried to forget but never would.

The family was deep into traditions, and holidays remained the same, even without Guiseppe. Angelina would prepare weeks in advance for *La Vigilia*, the feast of the Seven Fishes on Christmas Eve. In anticipation of this religious holiday, the sisters and Rose would cook, bake, and set up the Nativity Scene, called the *Presepio* in Italian. Christmas Eve supper usually included *Insalata di Mare* (seafood salad), *zuppi di vongole* (clams), *baccala* (salt cod), *gamberetti all'olio* (shrimp in garlic), baked eel, *scungilli* in tomato sauce over linguini, calamari (squid), and more.

But the best part of the evening was when the families came back from attending midnight mass. As the older children eagerly opened up their presents, the adults would gather around the dining room table, this time to nibble on sweets and drink espresso. Desserts like hot *zeppoli* (fried dough with powdered sugar), *struffoli* (marble-size fried dough balls with honey and colorful candy sprinkles on top), Italian cookies, and fruit and nuts would grace the table.

Although their bellies were filled, they still had room to savor every delectable treat that followed. With only a few hours of sleep, this scene would be reenacted again to celebrate Christmas Day.

Chapter 7

THE GREAT MIGRATION

ONE BY ONE THE MAIDAS WERE LEAVING Brooklyn for greener pastures. The talk in the neighborhood was that the bridge they were building would connect Brooklyn to Staten Island. It might even be named after an Italian explorer, Giovanni da Verrazano. But before the bridge became a reality, family members turned their attention to other places and directions.

The eldest son, Bruno, moved his wife and young son Tony to New Rochelle in Westchester County to take a job with a pharmaceutical company. The eldest daughter, Mary, moved to Long Island with her husband Paul and their three young daughters. Then the youngest daughter, Catherine, decided to move there too. She told Johnny, "I can't stand my in-laws; they are making my life miserable. Joe wants to move to the Island, and I think it's a good idea. What do you think?"

"Gee, Katy I hate to see you move so far. Mom will miss you, and Rose and I will, too. But if you think that's the best for your family, what can I say? I hope Joe is drinking less these days." Catherine didn't want her brother to know that her husband could sometimes be abusive to her, especially when he drank.

"I can handle him," was her reply. He didn't quite know what she meant by that.

Birds were leaving the nest. It was inevitable, since marriage and family were high on people's priority list after school, the service, and getting a job. The occasional "spinster" or "bachelor" in the neighborhood were always looked on with some pity. "Oh poor Emma, she never found a husband, eh?," they said, as though Emma really should have looked harder or settled for whoever would have her. Marriage was the way it was meant to be. Angelina still had daughters Anna and Teresa living in the neighborhood. Tessie, as everyone called her, had married a hot-headed Sicilian with whom she had two small daughters. Their marriage was punctuated by more fights than boxer Rocky Marciano ever imagined.

The next-to-eldest daughter, Anna, lived next door with her husband, Vinny, who was a liquor salesman, and their son, Robert. They enjoyed a full life that included dining at the famous Lundy's in Sheepshead Bay every Friday night and taking an occasional trip to the Catskills or Florida. But after Anna had a miscarriage, her nervous personality became more pronounced. She was an over-the-top clean freak, and it wasn't unusual to see little Anna cleaning at all hours of the night. If you wanted every inch of your house cleaned until it shined, gleamed, and squeaked, Anna would do it, all 4 foot 8 inches of her.

Other than Tessie and Anna's daily quick visits ("Hiya, Ma...d'ya need anything?"), Angelina was by herself, feeling lonely, especially in the late hours of the night. She attended

Mass frequently and spent Friday nights at the Youth Center playing bingo with the other ladies from the church group. And so Angelina quietly sat by as her children left the house and the neighborhood.

She wished it wasn't happening, but she understood it. After all, she herself had left her family in Italy when she was a girl. She'd be a hypocrite to say anything negative. Giuseppe, her devoted husband, had always told her their job would be to raise good sons and daughters and watch them have good lives of their own. She never imagined she would be doing it alone. Thankfully, her days were filled with visits from her friends Gilda and Sadie and her sisters Ida and Adeline. One by one the women would drop by, which eventually resulted in a colorful gab-fest.

Ida was a tall, robust woman, with dark, black hair, and she wore deep red lipstick. She was frequently referred to as "the gifted one," because she would read Tarot cards, predict the future, and tell stories from the old country. While stuffing her mouth with little pastries, she would dramatically wave her hands, gesticulating wildly. Her punch lines were delivered in Italian, just in case one of Angelina's grandchildren was present. Laughter would then fill the room, as the conversation and storytelling continued. Angelina refreshed the diminutive white and gold demitasse cups with freshly brewed espresso, making sure that the anisette bottle was on the table.

With each passing year, Angelina's health deteriorated, and she became more dependent on sons Johnny and Ernie. Riddled with arthritis and diabetes, her legs ached if she stood too long by the stove. That's when she decided that she should ask one of her sons if he would be interested in buying her house, on one condition—she went with it.

Which one of my daughters-in-law would be agreeable to this, she wondered. Ernie declined his mother's offer, with potential problems from his wife's in-laws. So when Ernie had the opportunity to buy a brand-new house in Staten Island, complete with a yard, trees, and plenty of space for his two small daughters to each have a room of their own, he decided to make the break and move out of Brooklyn.

For his part, Johnny told Rose, "Angel, what a great opportunity for us. It's helping us out as well as Ma, and we have the rents from the upstairs apartments for extra income." So it came to pass that the family moved into the three-level brownstone on 64th Street. Angelina had the space in the basement that consisted of a kitchen and dining room for family gatherings and friends. Over the years, another kitchen had been installed on the main level, which Rose and John and the girls could utilize. John wouldn't think of his mother sleeping in the basement though, and he insisted she sleep in the second bedroom that was next to theirs. His two daughters would share a small room in the front of the house, which was a sun porch at one time.

In the evenings Angelina would hobble up the back stairs, sit at the kitchen table, and listen to her two granddaughters' dialogue. Because of the age difference between Paula and Marian, she could frequently hear them squabble— they were always at odds with each other, it seemed. While Marian was still young enough to be playing with Barbie dolls, she seemed to derive great pleasure in snooping on her older sister. "Did that," "did not," "go away," "stop bugging me," "cut that out," "I'm gonna tell daddy on you," and so it went. Finally, disgusted with their antics, Angelina would utter something in Italian and shuffle off to bed with her rosary beads in hand. She always kept them in a pocket of her housecoat with a freshly washed handkerchief that she embellished with a hand-crocheted border.

This living arrangement left little privacy; the bedrooms were so close to each other you could easily hear someone pass gas, or get up to go to the bathroom. One evening, John was in an amorous mood. "Angel, come on, let's."

"No, babe, not tonight."

It didn't take much time for Paula to figure out what was going on. Brazenly, she opened her parents' bedroom door and yelled, "Mommy, do it for Daddy!" Quickly rushing back into her bed where her younger sister slept soundly, she pulled the covers over her head and tightly shut her eyes.

Chapter 8

RELATIVES

THE LATE 1950S AND EARLY 1960S were wonderful years for the family. Rose volunteered to work on the presidential campaign for a young Democrat. Enamored with his good looks, she talked about him constantly. If John Kennedy had lost the election, she would have been devastated. She met him once when he was campaigning in Brooklyn, and her heart raced. The night he won the election they celebrated at campaign headquarters.

John's sister Tessie was now living in an apartment upstairs. They'd moved back to a three-room apartment just across the hall from their original one. Tessie realized she was now the sole breadwinner and caregiver for her husband, Andy. He had been acting strangely and was diagnosed with a brain tumor. Having undergone a nine-hour operation, the left side of his face was distorted and his speech was slightly impaired. It was a miracle that he had even survived the operation, and he came home to recuperate.

Occasionally, Rose and John would hear Tessie raise her voice. "How am I gonna manage, Andrew? The girls need clothes for school. Ann needs books for college. Why did this have to happen? Why?" Then she'd break down, crying.

"Tessie, please . . . I'll get better . . . they'll give me my job back . . ."

She'd cry out, "You're a salesman! Your voice is gone. You can't make those calls anymore . . . you can't climb all those subway stairs . . . !" Then their voices would become muffled. John felt miserable for his sister, so when the tenant moved out, he offered that apartment to her. Financially and emotionally stressed, Tessie needed all the family support she could get.

Like most young girls in their early teens, Paula liked to hang out with her older cousins. If she approached Andrea and Ann on a good day, they would allow her to tag along with them to their friends' homes to watch "American Bandstand" on TV. Dancing was a popular pastime for teenagers, and the Philadelphia Lindy hop was all the rage. During the hot summer months, the young cousins would all schlep on the Number 4 subway train to visit Coney Island Beach. Anna's only son Robert (Bobby) was a devilishly good-looking young man. With his thick, dark, wavy brown hair and slim physique, he could pass for a teen idol. And when he turned eighteen his parents gave him a bright red Chevy Impala. Needless to say, Bobby was always in the company of pretty girls—Paula kept close tabs on her cousin. She adored his parents, and she considered Bobby more like her older brother.

John would look at his daughter Paula both approvingly and with some frustration. "My God, look at how grown-up you're getting," he'd say when she emerged from the bedroom all "gussied up" as he'd call it, in a pretty new dress with a little make-up on. But he drew the line at any boys meeting her anywhere but right there in their own home.

"Any kid who's good enough for my daughter is good enough to meet me!" Johnny would exclaim.

The dating years were stressful for John. It wasn't enough that he walked the streets of Manhattan every working day in the daylight hours. Now his daughter was causing him to walk the streets of Brooklyn at night. Paula had a difficult time keeping a curfew, so John would go out looking for her. Finally spotting her with Vinny, Benny, or Mickey, he would take her arm, look sternly at the young man, say nothing, put his fist in his mouth as if he were taking a bite out of his hand, and bring her home. "What am I gonna do with you, Paula?" he would ask.

"Buy me a cream soda and a slice of pizza," was her reply. It wasn't the answer he was looking for, but he would smile. She knew how to play the strings to his heart.

Having a teenage daughter with college years ahead was an expensive proposition. So without telling his family, John decided to supplement his income on the weekends selling real estate. He aced the exams and soon starting working Saturdays and Sundays for Rinaldi Realty. In the beginning it was tough, but he liked his boss, who seemed to be a fair and generous guy. And working for him had some small perks. Like the evening he came home with two brown paper bags. "Hey, Angel, look what Frank Rinaldi gave me!" he said, grinning from ear to ear.

Rose smiled at seeing the bundle he was so proudly carrying. Inside the bags were two dozen chick lobsters, little ones less than a pound each. Smiling never came naturally to Rose, but John always brought out the best in her. "Babe, are you working for food or money?" she asked teasingly.

"Hey, a working man's gotta eat!" he chided. "Now, woman, get busy and cook these beauties."

The Maidas all loved seafood, and lobsters were expensive. Paula and Marian watched transfixed as the lobsters crawled on top of each other in the big white cast iron sink. Rose swiftly cut lots of garlic and sautéed it in hot oil, opened cans of tomatoes, and added seasonings. Quickly she pulled the big spaghetti pot out of the cabinet and boiled the water.

When John came out of the bathroom, all cleaned up and smelling of Old Spice cologne, his nostrils inhaled the fragrant bouquet of the sauce simmering on top of the stove.

"*Lobster fra diavolo!*" he exclaimed, mimicking a waiter as he draped a dish towel over his arm. Twenty minutes later, they sat down to a feast of lobsters over linguine. "Mmmm . . . ." "Great . . ." "Mmmm . . ." They all kept eating and licking their fingers.

By the time Paula graduated from high school, she had no interest in going to college out of town, and John didn't push her. He thoroughly enjoyed having his daughter at home. Instead, she attended a girls' junior college in Brooklyn Heights. It was common in those days for girls to become a secretary, nurse, teacher, or better yet, get a coveted "MRS." degree.

Chapter 9

THE "D" WORD

WITH TWO YEARS OF COLLEGE AND SOME SEC-
RETARIAL courses thrown in, Paula felt ready to
take on the business world. The truth was that although she
disliked steno, her typing skills were fast. With graduation
day soon approaching in the spring, she was determined to
find a position in New York City. As it turned out, the place-
ment counselor at school called her into the office and told
her about a job that was available. "Paula, I just received a
phone call from Chilean Nitrate Sales Corporation. They
are looking to fill a secretarial position for a sales manager.
Interested?"

"Sure, most definitely. Just tell me where, when, and who
to call," she said enthusiastically.

The next day, wearing her Marlo Thomas look as in the
TV show *That Girl*—a straight skirt with a boxy suit jacket,
and her mid-length brown hair in a flip—Paula took the
subway into the city for her first official job interview. She
looked down at the piece of paper to check the address:
120 Broadway. Arriving ten minutes early, she stopped
in the ladies room to check her appearance. Not bad, she

thought. The receptionist told her to have a seat. "I'll advise Mr. Mooney you're here for your appointment," the woman said in a nicely officious manner.

As she tried to make herself comfortable, anxiety got the better of Paula. Oh, jeez!, she wondered. So much for entering the business world, what am I doing here?" Her hands were beginning to sweat, and as she opened her purse to find a handkerchief to dry them, a voice welcomed her. When she looked up, she was gazing into a pair of hazel eyes and a face that made her legs feel like Jell-O.

"Hi, my name is Tom Mooney. You must be Paula."

Wow! What a cutie, she thought. He had a Bobby Kennedy sort of look, clean cut with light brown hair and a slim physique. He was wearing a well-tailored brown suit, with an orange silk pocket handkerchief.

Escorting her into a conference room with a large mahogany table and red leather chairs around it, he said "Paula, please take a seat," and then he proceeded to tell her something of his life. Perhaps he did this because he could sense her uneasiness, but she wasn't sure. He said he was born and raised in St. Louis, Missouri, graduated from the University of Notre Dame, earned a Master's Degree from Washington University, lived in Larchmont, and was married and had children. She heard him say, "Now tell me something about you."

Shucks, she thought, feeling instantly deflated. Her mind was racing, as she told herself, calm down, Paula, keep it cool, and don't start to stammer: "Well, I'm just finishing Junior College. I live in Brooklyn with my family. And I'm embarking on a career in business."

"Can you type and take dictation?" he asked.

"Of course," she replied.

"How about taking a letter now?" he suggested. Thank God, he dictated at a deliberate, even pace. To her delight, she seemed to have gotten every word. When she read it back, he said, "That's fine." The interview lasted more than an hour. "If you're offered the position, could you start immediately?"

"Oh no, I'm graduating in two weeks and then a few girlfriends from school and I are going to Florida for a vacation." Probably not a good thing to blurt out, she thought after she said it.

With that, she got up to leave and he extended his hand, saying, "I'll get in touch with you, and thank you for coming."

The next day all of her friends at school were inquiring how the interview went. She told her closest friend, " Laila, he had this incredible smile, and his eyes . . . but heck he's married."

"Do you think you'll get the job" she asked.

"I'm not sure. We talked a lot if that means anything," Apparently it did mean something, because a week later she received a letter. It read, "Dear Ms. Maida, This will confirm our pleasant discussion today. We are pleased to offer you a secretarial position in our Iodine Sales Department to be effective June twenty-seventh, at the salary level we discussed. We would appreciate hearing from you as soon as possible if you accept our offer so that we may hold this position for you. Very truly yours, T. F. Mooney."

She stared at his neat, purposeful signature, "T.F. Mooney." Ecstatic and a tad bit surprised that she landed the job; even better, he was willing to wait for her, and the salary was more than adequate. When she told her father the good news, he was thrilled.

"Paula, you worked hard at school, and your mother and I see no reason why you shouldn't go to Florida with your friends after graduation. It will be your graduation present," he offered, the newly proud father of a working girl.

Five perky girls from Brooklyn landed in Miami with suntan lotion and bikinis, looking for fun and adventure. It wasn't hard to find it with water skiing lessons with a handsome instructor, lying on the beach during the day, and drinking and dancing at night. It only served to reinforce an idea that Paula had been toying with. For months Paula had been intrigued with the thought of becoming a Playboy Bunny. She had never mentioned it to anyone, but ever since high school graduation this idea was percolating in her mind. And fortuitously there was a Playboy Club in Miami. She was familiar with the Bunny concept, since her oldest cousin Tony was one of the managers of the Playboy Club in New York City.

Tony was a good-looking guy, swaggeringly self-confident, with dark hair and natty clothes, sort of like a young John Travolta. Pretty women were always flocking around him. When Tony heard that Paula, her date, and two other couples were taking a limo into the city to go to the Copacabana on prom night, he suggested they stop by the Playboy Club at 60th Street and Fifth Avenue. Who could resist an invite to the Playboy Club? The guys thought the Bunnies were hot, but to Paula's thinking they were a lot more than that. They were sophisticated, gorgeous, and worldly.

Tanning in the Miami sun for hours gave her ample time to think about career choices. Why not go for it?, she thought, I'm here. Persistence prevailed, and she actually got an interview (it didn't hurt for her to mention Tony's name). Taking her friend Laila along for support, they drove to the Miami Playboy Club in the budget car they rented for the week. The thrill of going to a Playboy Club was exciting for an eighteen-year-old girl, as her heart was pounding with anticipation. Paula was surprised to see other girls there. Apparently this was an open casting day. The Bunny Mother, a tall red head with a turned up nose, must have been in her mid-thirties, Paula surmised. She was very cordial, and before long the woman asked some of the girls (including Paula) to try on Bunny outfits, complete with rabbit ears, high heels, cotton tail, and cleavage.

Talk about feeling sexy! Paula looked into the mirror and felt powerful; definitely not a teenage girl anymore, but a woman. The red and white polka-dot bikini she had taken to Florida never made her body look this good. She chose a white Bunny costume to show off her golden tan. The high heels and the hi-cut of the outfit elongated her legs. She looked taller than her 5'4"frame. How do they construct these little outfits was her immediate thought. I'm going to be a Playboy Bunny in Miami. Screw secretarial work.

Paula was bubbling with anticipation. But she had one obstacle to overcome. Calling home the next day with a big smile in her voice, and hidden agenda on her mind, she blurted out, "Hi Daddy, I'm having a wonderful time. The weather is sunny and we go swimming every day." In her sweetest voice, she added, "And guess what, Daddy? I have another job offer."

When she told her father of her plan, he was enraged, and she could picture him biting his lower lip and waving his hand as he said, "Don't even think about it, Paula, that's an obscene job for a young woman. If you don't get your butt back to Brooklyn, I will personally fly down and drag you back, get it?" Case closed.

The relationship Paula had with her father was based on love, not fear. Even when she was a child and he tried to discipline her by frightening her with the snapping sound of his leather belt, she knew he would never hit her. It was all for show. The worst thing that ever happened to her was once she answered her mother back, and her dad put soap in her mouth, or at least he tried. She never talked back to her mother again. Paula knew her Johnny adored her, and the feeling was returned. Of course, she would fly back. Did she really have a choice?

It's funny how different choices can lead to an entirely different journey for people. With an odd mixture of regret and anticipation, Paula flew back home to Brooklyn. Perhaps going back to a secretarial position wouldn't be so terrible, she tried to rationalize. Wasn't she elated when she first got the offer? But that was prior to going to Miami. Now she had an opportunity to be a Playboy Bunny. Hands down, being a Bunny was more glamorous than a secretary, and the pay was more. She had heard about the generous tips the Bunnies received. But she hated incurring her father's disapproval. He acted as any caring, respectable man of his day would. On the other hand, she was not sure he would have felt the same had he known what was coming next.

The first day on the job, Paula consoled herself. At least her new boss was good-looking. As the first year passed, Paula's secretarial skills improved and her attraction to Tom Mooney grew. It started nonchalantly with lunch dates, and then it progressed to dinners. Tom eventually confided to Paula that he was unhappy in his home life and that his marriage was unsatisfying to him. He said, although he and his wife stayed together for the children's sake, they were leading separate lives. But the fact remained, Tom was still legally married. Confused, but certain for her feelings for him, Paula thought it best to look for another position. She found one with a Wall Street firm as an administrative assistant to the director of the foreign department. But because of her reluctance to leave her job with Tom, she initially declined the company's offer. It was only when they came back with a substantial increase in salary, that Paula knew she would be a fool to decline this position a second time. Certain that she and Tom would eventually work things out together, their only other obstacles were her parents. Would they accept Tom into the family?

Mothers seem to have a sixth sense when it comes to their children. Early on, Rose suspected her daughter had a thing for her good-looking boss, but she thought it was a harmless crush. Meanwhile, Tom and Paula continued to see each other after work and once they even ventured on a business trip together. But Paula had a cunning idea, or so she thought. She had persuaded Tom to go along with her plan, which was to introduce Tom to her parents using another name. He would be Matt Kidder to her family. She knew if she brought him home as Tom Mooney they would immediately dislike him. Using an alias would give them time to get to know how kind and generous a man Tom was. At least there would be nothing to prejudice their opinion of him. After all, how could they not see what she saw in him? He was educated, well-spoken, and handsome.

Sure enough, they were delighted to meet him. They were at their best; gracious, loquacious, generous in the amounts of food they offered, and with the special bottle of wine they'd opened to make their own good impression. Paula was happy but she was also miserable. Tom went along with her charade, but giving him this fake identity felt weird to both of them. Finally after a month of this drama, she had to speak up. The guilt was weighing on her.

Now was the time to break the news to her parents. After dinner one evening, she mustered up the courage and said, "I have something important to tell you." From the tone of her voice and the expression on her face, her father told his younger daughter, Marian, to please leave the room. She reluctantly scampered out of the room, purposely leaving the door open so she could eavesdrop. "Mom, Dad, Matt Kidder is not really Matt."

Rose looked at her daughter with piercing eyes and said, "He's Tom Mooney, isn't he?" The truth was out, filling the air with the loudest damning silence. There were no hysterics, no raised voices.

John asked, "Why are you telling us now?"

"Because I love him," Paula answered, her eyes filling with tears at the sharp sense of guilt she felt. "We want to get married eventually, and I want you both to be at our wedding." She subsequently told them that Tom was planning to go to Mexico for a divorce. There were no fireworks. If anything, there seemed to be relief that the truth was finally out.

Rose expressed concern about what she would tell her family. "How can I tell them you're marrying a divorced man?" she asked, her own eyes filling with tears. The D word, divorce, was not acceptable in those days. Moreover, he had children. My God, this was serious.

John added, "We like Tom. But we can't be happy about this for either of you. I know you, sweetheart. You'll do what you're gonna do, whether we like it or not. We'll be at your wedding or you'll just get married without us." He paused, shaking his head in frustration. "And I couldn't stand that."

A year later, on a hot summer day in July, Paula and Tom wed in Judge Landy's home in Queens, New York. The entourage included her parents, sister, the best man and maid of honor. After the ceremony, they all went to the Tavern on the Green for dinner. Sitting under the stars, and enjoying the warmth of the day, Paula was ecstatic to be Mrs. Thomas F. Mooney. Her father, on the other hand, was a portrait of mixed emotions—pain, pride, conflict, and love. He gave his daughter away and graciously paid for the dinner and champagne, but he had sadness in his eyes. This was not the wedding he envisioned for his daughter.

Dancing with her father, Paula instinctively knew that when he put his strong arms around her, regardless of what her Johnny felt inside, she would always have his unwavering love. He said, "You are so special to me, Paula. Be happy. If Tom isn't good to you, just come home, sweetheart."

Little did Paula realize that her parents must have been reminded of their own wedding day. With a grateful heart, she thanked her parents for supporting her decision to marry this man. But most of all, she thanked her Johnny for being there.

Chapter 10

PERIOD OF
ADJUSTMENT

ITALIANS ARE FAMOUS FOR HOLDING GRUDGES. A number of relatives will tell you, with astonishing emotion still reverberating, what slight they encountered fifty years ago.

"That schemer . . . he knew he'd never repay me." "The way she flirted with my husband, I hope she rots in hell." "Me? Talk to them? Those cheapskates?"

Rose and John were not interested in carrying on these traditions. They left the newlyweds alone as long as they possibly could. But after they returned home from a honeymoon in Bermuda, John had to call. "How ya doin', honey?" he asked.

"Fine, Daddy, just fine. I miss you. How's Mom doing?"

"We're both fine, Paula. It isn't easy accepting this, but we're gonna try."

"Oh, Daddy, I can't ask for anything more. You'll see. Tom will be a wonderful husband and son-in-law."

"Why don't you two come for dinner Friday night?" he asked.

"We'll be there, Daddy! I'll bring dessert."

And so it went. In the ensuing months and years, Rose and John genuinely learned to care deeply for their son-in-law. Tom's winning personality, his competitive nature, and Irish sense of humor couldn't help but endear them to him. Paula and Tom lived in a one-bedroom apartment in Jersey City and were both working on Wall Street for different firms. When Paula came home, she loved cooking and showing Tom her best domestic side. She assumed this was an Italian trait that all girls get from their mothers. And their lovemaking left nothing to be desired. There were days when she didn't need a train to commute—she could have floated to work.

Since more than half of Tom's salary was going to child support and alimony, a dinner invitation was never turned down. "Tom, we want you to taste an Italian version of corned beef and cabbage." "Paula, your mother bought so much fish, we'll never finish it. Why don't you and Tom come over?" "Hi, you two, Aunt Adeline is making homemade pasta to bring over. Why don't you come for dinner tomorrow night?"

Aside from the always-delicious meals, John enjoyed talking sports, politics, and Wall Street with Tom. Then, as though it had just occurred to him, before the couple departed for home, he would always say, "Do you need any groceries? Come to my cantina."

Rose and John had gotten into the habit of using a small storage room in the basement as their own mini-grocery store. The shelves were filled with canned goods, boxes of macaroni, paper towels, cans of coffee, and bags of flour.

Paula gladly obliged, first because it made her father happy, and second because it was free. As they drove off, John would yell, "Call us when you get home."

Tom grew up in the Midwest, and as an only child of older parents, he was constantly amused by the working dynamics of an Italian-American family. "Do you always have to shout at each other when you're eating dinner?" he would ask his wife.

"No, Tom, we are not shouting, we are talking."

Or, "What's this kissing thing? Do I have to kiss everyone I meet in your family?" "Yes, Tom, you do!"

A year and a half later, Paula informed her family that she was expecting. "I'm gonna be a grandfather! Can you believe it? My daughter is having a baby! Rose, did ya hear? A baby!"

Rose looked at him deadpan. "Really? No, Johnny, tell me again."

"Yeah, and that means you are going to be a grandmother . . ."

Paula's relationship with Tom was loving and secure. Although money was tight, they had saved enough, and with a small loan from Tom's mother in St. Louis, they purchased a three-bedroom home on a corner lot in the town of New Providence. Several months later, Paula gave birth to a five-pound, fourteen ounce baby boy. No one was surprised when it was announced that the new baby would be named John. Paula liked the sound of John Bryan and the way it looked on paper. She would call him JB for short, and she knew it would please her father, naming the baby after him.

Looking more Italian than Irish, the baby had a mop of silky black hair, and dark eyes that looked like small black olives. His grandparents acted as if there never was, nor ever would be, a more beautiful, more important infant in the entire world. Clothing, a crib, layettes, and diaper service were all gifts from them. They also gave Paula the giant gift of freedom. "Anytime you need a babysitter, we'll be here."

That said, it wasn't long before it became obvious that the long drive from Brooklyn to New Jersey was bothering John. Across a river and over the Goethals Bridge was geographically too far to suit him. "Paula, by the time we get here, the baby is older!" he would smilingly grumble upon arriving.

"Oh, Dad, it's only an hour. Gives us that much more time to miss you."

Nonetheless, their talk eventually turned to relocating to New Jersey. There were pros—but there were two big cons. John was still working for the Postal Service in New York City. Because he was so sentimental, leaving his family home would stir up major emotions. Rose, on the other hand, relished the idea of having her very own house. All those years she had lived in her mother-in-law's house. Wouldn't it be nice to have a home that she herself could select?

Chapter 11

WE PLAN—
GOD LAUGHS

THE YEARS THAT FOLLOWED WERE FILLED WITH LOVE and family activities. Some summers were spent on Cape Cod, where Tom's children, who were now residing in St. Louis, would join the growing Maida clan. A noticeable degree of contentment seemed to hover over all of them. Paula and Tom had moved into a center hall colonial in Short Hills after JB turned one year old. Tom was doing quite well as a chemical analyst, and he was often interviewed and quoted in *The Wall Street Journal*. Other trade papers featured "Mooney on Money," and listened to what this young man had to say about the chemical industry. Tom also arranged trips to Europe for his associates and their clients to visit companies, and wives were always invited to go along.

Chalk it up to a growing level of sophistication, but the more Paula traveled and saw other places, the more interested she became in houses—what style they were and how they were decorated. She would enthusiastically give her parents a detailed account of their travels abroad and the architecture of the homes and castles she had visited.

She was developing a passion for decorating and had a good eye for remembering what she saw. In due time, she realized that decorating and selling houses might be an interesting combination. Since her baby was born, she had become a full-time, stay-at-home mom, so getting a real estate license seemed to make sense. Knowing that she was weak in math, and realizing that calculators were not allowed during the exam, she enlisted the aid of her father to coach her. "Paula, don't worry, you can ace this exam. If I passed, so can you."

"Dad, you're a wiz at math, I'm not." Eventually after two attempts and help from her father, she succeeded.

Paula enjoyed decorating the colonial house and thought it would sell quickly so they could turn a nice profit. She persuaded Tom to put the house on the market, knowing that financially they could afford a nicer home. And now with a real estate license, she could search for her dream house. Working part-time as a real estate agent, it didn't take Paula long to find her next decorating project. She liked working for two long-time residents of the area, Phyllis and Connie Grill. The Grill sisters knew every street in Short Hills and all the gossip that went along with each home. They warned Paula of the local country clubs that did not accept Jews, Italians, and African Americans. "What, in this day and age?" Paula responded, finding discrimination appalling.

But there it was, her dream house. It was open house day for multiple listings in Short Hills when Paula came across One Twin Oak Road, a grand old English Tudor set high on a knoll. She knew a house of this scale and size would be the envy of all their friends, and it would be wonderful home where they could entertain. The location was ideal—a short walk to the train station for Tom and to school for JB. It whispered "Ralph Lauren Style," even before that decorating term was coined. Yes, it was definitely a "trophy house."

With three sets of French doors in the living room, high beamed ceilings, leaded glass windows, and a large square living room with a huge bay window, she could visualize the room entirely decorated. Filling the space with an ebony baby grand piano right there, to showcase Tom's talent at the piano, it was a house meant to be filled up with friends and family.

For the first time, Paula made a decision without enlisting the opinion of her father.

When they were in escrow, she brought Rose and John to view the property. "Why do three people need such a big house?" was John's instinctive response.

She knew what he was thinking; he had grown up in a family of ten people in close quarters. Quickly, she responded, "Gee, Dad, it's a good investment, don't you think?" Remembering her grandparents' garden in Brooklyn, she added, "Did you see the rose garden in the back?" Her creative juices flowing, her mind racing, Paula reassured her father that with so much space they could even have their own bedroom and bath during visits to Short Hills. Heck, they could even live there someday if they wanted.

With everything going so well, Paula couldn't tell if it was an Italian thing, or human thing, but she was beginning to feel uneasy. She enjoyed having such a beautiful home, but she couldn't shake this feeling. Every once in awhile, she would recall what her grandmother used to say. "Nobody can be too happy for too long." Negative thinking is so toxic, which Paula knew. But why was she feeling so cautious these days?

Recalling what her father used to say about his wife came into her mind. "Paula, your mom must be a witch because she can sense things before they happen." Was what she was feeling a premonition of things to come?

On a cold winter morning while lying in bed with Tom, as she gazed out of the big leaded glass windows, Paula quietly whispered to Tom, "I hope our life never changes, and nothing ever breaks our bubble. We are so fortunate, our life is so perfect." She knew she had much to be thankful for and was grateful for all they had. She thanked God in her prayers every night. It seemed to be working. And to make her life even sweeter, her father finally announced that after thirty years of working for the United States Postal Service, he was going to retire.

Her sister Marian married Wayne, and they moved to Staten Island. Renting a small apartment in a two-family house in Tottenville, they seemed to be content. Marian never aspired to the big dreams her sister envisioned for herself. They were a happy working couple saving to purchase their first house and eventually start a family.

When Paula found out that her father was finally considering retiring, she quickly set about finding a house for her parents to purchase in New Jersey. Her mother requested a country style house that had a fireplace and a nice eat-in kitchen. For Rose the thrill and prospect of having her own home and moving to the country was euphoric. Paula took them house hunting, and eventually they found a blue colonial house on Elm Street in Millburn. It was a small, comfortable house, with a corner fireplace in the living room. The dining room had pickled white pine wainscoting, and the kitchen had a little breakfast nook that overlooked a wooded backyard. Rose was hooked, and John was nervous.

After much deliberation, John submitted a bid. When their offer was accepted, John realized that he had no choice but to sell the family home. The time had come! His childhood home, his adulthood home, his parents' first home in America, had to be sold. As happy as Rose was with the prospect of a new house, John was conflicted about selling the old one. But, as fate would have it, a couple from Bari, Italy, who had several children and another one on the way made an offer on the house. John took this as a divine sign— an Italian family with young kids, just like his father and mother. With the knowledge that he was selling the house to people who really loved it, John Maida emotionally was able to make the move. On moving day, he and Rose said goodbye to neighbors they had known for decades, with John telling everyone that he was moving to Jersey where Paula and his grandson lived.

While Rose was thriving in her new home after a year or so, John was getting bored. He was only in his 50s and hadn't counted on his energy wanting to do more and keep going. One day, he informed his wife of an idea he was pondering. Rose thought it was stroke of genius. He announced that he wanted to go back to work, not selling real estate, but this time on Wall Street. He had spoken so often with Tom that he had become intrigued with the workings of that fascinating center of financial wizardry, chicanery, and fortunes quickly won and lost. While John didn't have a wheeling-dealing bone in his body, after working three decades in a very staid and predictable job he was ready for something fast paced and exciting.

With his mind made up and with Tom's assistance, John landed a job at Morgan Stanley, a prominent investment brokerage firm. With his quick math skills, he was a natural in their back offices underwriting department. Rose and John were now living a different life in suburbia. Rose would drive John to the train station in the morning and pick him up at night. Cocktails, conversation, and Rosie's cooking were waiting for him at home. Life was good!

The bubble began to burst that fall. Tom was forty-one, slim, and in excellent physical shape. He was a runner, a golfer, and a vitamin junkie. But in the preceding few months, he'd been getting sick a lot. He had colds, fevers, back pains, and recently, blood in his urine. After Tom had a complete medical work up, his doctor suggested some additional testing in the hospital. At first they suspected tuberculosis. Despite interminable testing, the doctors kept on asking Paula, "How much does your husband smoke?"

It was exasperating for her. "I've told you, he doesn't smoke," she repeated over and over. She was sick with worry, and couldn't let Tom see how anxious she was feeling. Her exasperation soon turned into devastation. Tom was diagnosed with adeonocarcinoma in the lungs. It hit her like a ton of bricks.

"What? What do you mean? What are you telling me?" Lung cancer—Tom had lung cancer and had never smoked a day in his life. When she finally comprehended what the doctors were telling her, Paula visited her parents. As she broke the unimaginable news, Rose started weeping; John was shaken, biting his lower lip.

Paula tried to remember everything the doctors had told her privately, and in between sobbing she blurted out, "They don't know . . . a few months . . . they don't know!"

John gave his clean-ironed handkerchief to his daughter to wipe the tears from her eyes. "Honey, we will do everything we can to help you, to help Tom. You won't be alone."

He always seemed to say the right words at the right time. He was tender, gentle, loving.

John was not going to let his daughter go through this ordeal by herself. Not as long as he was still standing.

Tom's illness took center stage, as all of their lives and schedules soon adjusted to what needed to be done. It didn't matter what time of day or night it was. Ask anyone whose life has been touched by cancer. You get to know the drill: the bad chemo days, the emergency room visits, the weight loss, hair loss, the excruciating pain and degradation—and fear as you begin to lose the battle.

Then came that final evening when a blood clot took Tom's life. It was a miserable chilly, bleak day in February. Paula had been sitting by Tom's bedside in the hospital, and she thought he was sleeping. The heart monitor made a strange beeping sound, so she immediately called the nurse. In a matter of moments, he was pronounced dead.

Paula's brain understood it, but it didn't make sense. "My husband is gone. Tom is dead. Our son is only eight years old, he needs a father. He is too young to die." Then she recalled what her grandmother used to say, "nobody can be too happy for too long." As she walked out of his hospital room, eyes red and swollen from crying, gazing at the floor, a hand touched her arm. It was her Johnny. She wept in his arms. "Daddy, what do I do now?"

Chapter 12

STARTING OVER

N O MATTER HOW LOST AND ALONE PAULA FELT AT TIMES, she knew she could count on her parents to be there for her. Her father was her rock. "Don't worry about a thing, honey, I'll take care of everything." How she needed to know that. Her head wouldn't stop hurting. Her son look confused. How had her wonderful life fallen apart like this? It was just a year ago she was having dinner parties at Twin Oaks. Even Twin Oaks was gone.

The cancer changed their lives; she kept on thinking, "I want my old life back." When Tom began feeling ill, requiring a constant round of doctor visits, the decision to sell the house and rent an apartment in New York City seemed like a sensible way to go. They sought out the best doctors and medical care, and living in Manhattan would make the commute to work easier for Tom. From the apartment they rented, Wall Street was a short bus ride away. The Pavilion, located on East 77th Street and York Avenue, had many nice features, including doormen. In inclement weather they could hail a taxi for Tom. They all were aware of his health situation and were extremely solicitous. It was so obvious, one day a healthy good-looking man, and in several months a gaunt fellow with no hair, having to use a cane.

Thankfully there was a public school just across the street, PS#7, where Paula enrolled JB. What's more, there was a park down the street where he could play with his new friend Craig, who lived in the building with his divorced mother. In the short time the three Mooneys lived there, they got the feel for city living. In fact, Paula was getting to know a few of her neighbors, and she learned that two famous personalities resided in the building. Both comedian Rodney Dangerfield and Bishop Fulton J. Sheen had apartments there—two men who were so completely opposite. Sometimes the elevator doors would open and she would find herself exchanging polite conversation with them about the weather or such.

Now that Tom was gone, Paula couldn't help but feel that he was still there. She would look at the clock, and think . . . he would be coming home now; we would be sitting down to dinner. But he wouldn't be walking through the front door. He would never be there; she would feel the crushing weight of reality all over again. Tom was gone from her life.

The world seemed to become a haze through which she was moving. Thankfully, Paula had her Johnny. "Sweetheart, how would you like to handle the funeral arrangements for Tom?" Her father involved her only to the extent he thought she could handle it.

"I don't know, Dad, where do I start?

John immediately called Rose's cousin, Eddie the undertaker. The Marasco Funeral Home was a family business from the time they'd immigrated to America, with their first funeral home at 177 Sullivan Street in New York City. Eddie came to the apartment to pick up the clothes Tom would be dressed in for the viewing. Paula selected Tom's favorite formal attire, a single-breasted charcoal gray velvet suit, a burgundy bow tie with a never-worn white dress shirt, and black patent leather shoes. The guy had style, and with his trim physique, he wore clothes well. "Tom always looked handsome, Paula. He'd be pleased at the care you're taking of him now," Eddie said softly.

"Thank you, Eddie," she replied, "My parents are doing a lot more than I am."

With the arrangements made, the young widow sat through the wake for three days and nights at the Frank E. Campbell Funeral home on Madison Avenue, an unconscionable amount of time by today's standards. Friends, relatives, and co-workers came to pay their last respects, while Tom's ex-wife and children sent their condolences but chose to remain in St. Louis. Paula overheard herself being referred to as the "Widow Mooney." "It's so tragic and unfair, so young and with a small child." When she heard their words, bitter tears and a lump formed in her throat. Tragic, unfair—what was she supposed to do with her eight-year-old son and her life now?

"Sweetheart, things look dark and bleak, but all this will change. You'll see. Someday you'll even remarry. You're young yet. Trust your old man. Don't buy a family plot. Just take care of Tom now."

"Ok, Dad, whatever you say, you're probably right." But she felt close to dead inside. When someone you love dies, you're caught up in a bizarre world, which seems like a strange planet where nothing is as it used to be. The deceased and you become center stage for a while, and then—"poof." He's buried, and you're supposed to get on with living. How, she wondered would she go on without Tom?

In the weeks after the funeral, Paula would find herself sitting for hours in the evening listening to Barry Manilow music, over and over. A glass of sherry, a glass or two of white wine, and then one of Tom's Valiums she had found in the medicine cabinet became routine before she could finally fall asleep. She wanted to erase the ugly memories of his illness, of her own emotions. She was sick of them. She was sick of sickness. She was sick of herself. Rose and John were beginning to worry about their daughter.

"You're getting too thin," her mom said. The joke in the family was that Paula could eat her father and brother-in-law under the table and never gain a pound. After two months of watching her behavior and weight loss, they had to find a solution to help her.

"Paula, Mom and I are coming into the city tonight to take you and JB out to dinner; we want to run an idea by you." The conversation began, "Paula, we've done a lot of thinking about your present situation. And we think we have a really good plan. How about if we buy a large house so that we could all live together? It sure makes sense to us."

"Wouldn't that be nice, dear?" Rose asked, with a look of gentle pleading in her eyes. "We could sell our house and all live together," she continued.

Paula thought for a few minutes, and turned to her son. "JB, what do you think? Would you like all of us to live together?"

His face had brightened at the very start of the conversation. "You mean live with you and Grandma and Grandpa?" he asked, wanting to be absolutely sure he'd gotten it right.

John quickly chimed in, "That's exactly what we mean. I have this crazy idea that you and I get along pretty well, huh?" JB loved his grandparents, and Paula could see his mind calculate the gives-and-gets of the plan.

"I'd have to change schools, wouldn't I?" he asked.

"Well, next semester, you would. But you'll really like your new school. I know you will," his grandmother answered.

Paula found herself quickly warming to their plan, but with a twist. "You're right, Mom, I need to be closer to you and Daddy. JB will be finishing his school year soon and we can move into an apartment not far from you."

"An apartment?" her mother asked.

"Yes. I think that's a good solution all the way around. You stay in your house. We move close to you." Paula's face relaxed into a smile.

John started to protest, but immediately Rose touched his arm lightly. "Babe, that's a good suggestion. Whatever Paula wants, at least they will be closer."

With that, John raised his glass of wine. "Here's to us and a new beginning!" he said. They clinked their glasses to toast, with JB sipping his Shirley Temple, anxiously trying to get to the Maraschino cherry at the bottom.

It was a good compromise for all of them. Paula still had an independent streak, and if she knew anything about herself, she knew she had to heal and move on. And what better way than with no risk attached? She loved the idea of having her family close, but not so close as under the same roof. Besides, her parents had spent too many years living with Grandma; they didn't need to have roommates once again. They needed their house to themselves; marriage had certainly reinforced that for her. While she never discussed it with them, she had the feeling that her folks still had a healthy sex life. They certainly patted and teased each other enough. Happy banter between couples is a good sign that can lead to happy endings, not all the time, but surely some of the time.

That June, after JB completed his school year, they moved back to New Jersey into a comfortable two-bedroom, garden-style apartment. They each had their own bathroom, which made her son especially happy. In Manhattan, he'd often roll his eyes at his mom's assortment of cosmetics, creams, and hair-rollers.

"Jeez, mom, there's no room for me," he'd understandably complain. Once Paula enrolled JB into elementary school for the fall semester, she had time to re-examine her life. She needed a plan and a job. She needed to find an identity. Without the Mr., there was no Mrs.

Chapter 13

ALL IN A DAY'S WORK

I T FELT AWKWARD FOR PAULA TO BE BACK in the suburbs as a widow. It's as though she had left home one morning, the beautiful home Tom and she had in Short Hills, only to arrive back a while later to an entirely changed life. Sometimes, she would hum those eerie first notes that introduced the *Twilight Zone*, "Doo-doo-doo doo . . ." She did it to amuse herself and to keep some perspective on feeling as though she had wandered into a very strange zone indeed. "Dad, I'm like a fish out of water," she said to him early on.

"Of course you are, honey. You're young, you're beautiful, and you have your whole life ahead of you. Would you rather be an old fart like your mother and me?" How could she not laugh? That was her Johnny. One way or other, he was determined to make her smile. He didn't tell her, but he missed Tom's presence and the conversations they used to share.

"Remember when Grandpa died?" he asked. Without waiting for an answer, he continued, "Grandma always wore black after that."

"Dad," Paula said playfully, "the fatter Grandma got, the thinner it made her look." "Be nice now," he'd counter. It was basically true about the mandatory years of mourning. In Brooklyn, all the old ladies wore black. They'd wear their hair in buns that sat like a frown on the back of their necks. Paula looked in the mirror and studied her face. Dad was right—she was young and still attractive. Besides, wearing a bun was not her style. She had a son to raise, and above all she needed an income.

Although she wasn't exactly broke, the small life insurance policy Tom left would only last so long. Thanks to the J&R Support System (the incomparable Johnny & Rose), she knew she had a safety net if she needed one. Weekly dinner with her folks always ended up the same way. First Rose, and then John. "Paula," Rose would say, sotto voce, "do you need anything?" With that, she'd thrust a $10 bill into her hand.

"No, Mom, I'm fine, honestly!" She would protest, attempting to give it back to her. "Don't say anything to your father."

Then John would walk his grandson out to the car, and before he could get in, he'd put a folded bill into his hand. When Paula noticed, John would say, "It's not for you, it's for JB." It was hopeless—and wonderful. It was like watching the same act all the time.

God knows, Johnny and Rose were not rich. But like many of her aunts and uncles, they were able to save money year after year. "If you can't pay for it," was an unwritten motto, "you don't buy it."

On his postal worker's salary, then as a realtor, and now with Morgan Stanley, John had managed to save enough to live in relative comfort. Their home was furnished tastefully. Neither of them cared a whole lot for staying up on fashion, so the clothes they had served them well. He owned a Buick Le Sabre with low mileage—it got him where he wanted to go. In their generation, necessities were exactly that. The whole idea of "status symbols" hadn't taken root, certainly not in middle class Italian families. A good leather bag was meant to be exactly that. Nobody's initials were seen anywhere on it. A car was transportation. Most commuters didn't drive more than a few miles to work or would park near their train. No wonder there always seemed to be money to spare.

Then one day, while reading the help wanted ads in the *New Jersey Star-Ledger*, Paula saw a listing that piqued her interest. A hotel in a nearby town was looking for someone to do advertising and promotional work for its restaurant and cocktail lounge, increase sales revenues, and enhance the hotel's visibility. "Am I qualified?" she wondered. "Probably not," came her own reply. But she applied anyway. Watching Tom ebb away had changed her thinking about life. "What the heck? What's the worst thing that could happen?"

She telephoned the hotel and was given an appointment with the general manager, Phil Columbo. Her anxiety was turning into excitement as she drove past the large stately homes and the beautiful rural setting leading to its entrance. The hotel was located in Morristown, about ten miles west from her home. Its location was near the historic site of a Revolutionary War battle and General Washington's headquarters. Nestled among these homes on a dead-end street, she could see the hotel tucked away in a large parking lot.

Within moments, she was escorted to the G.M.'s office, thinking, "Gee, I hope this guy's not some stuffy old codger, like the hotel." When she entered the room, his back was facing the wall as he spoke. He swiveled his chair around to the front of his desk and hung up the phone. To her delight, he said, "Hi, I'm Phil Columbo," in a friendly, welcoming voice. He bounded up from his desk chair, his hand outstretched. She shook his hand, remembering to take it firmly, with confidence.

"A pleasure to meet you, Mr. Columbo. I'm Paula Mooney."

"Most people call me Mr. C," he said, immediately making her feel at home. He gestured for her to sit in the chair across from him. Mr. C was in his mid-thirties, medium build, dark complexion, jet-black curly hair. He proved to be a down-to-earth guy who immediately made her feel comfortable. He was charming and a bit cocky, with a beautiful smile that reminded her of Dean Martin. Good-looking Italian men she understood.

That day, Paula made it a point to be stylishly dressed and look the part of an advertising executive. At least what she imagined one would look like. She had a nice figure and dressed to show it off appropriately, but modestly. She selected a dark brown, two-piece suit with a fitted jacket and straight skirt slightly below the knee, pearl earrings, crocodile heels, and a brown clutch purse; her wavy dark brown hair hung loosely, touching her shoulders. Her father would soon be arriving to pick up JB to take him to school. When he saw his daughter, he looked her over, and with an approving smile and wolf whistle, said, "Knock em' dead, sweetheart, you look super."

Mr. C cut a pretty dashing figure himself, well-groomed and wearing a perfectly fitted blue suit. After the perfunctory nice-to-meet-you, he cut right to the chase. With her resume in his hand, he said, "Now that I can put a person with the pages, I want to read this again." Paula could feel herself getting nervous, and her hands started to get clammy. "OK," he muttered softly, commenting aloud. "Oh yeah, husband— wow, sorry about that, young son, huh? Good . . . parents close by . . ." Then he looked up "What's your experience for this position?" he asked.

Here goes, she thought. She explained that she was the widow of a high-profile Wall Street executive, and she had entertained lavishly and done a fair amount of traveling. "I love people and throwing parties," she said, quite honestly. "Oh," and in a spontaneous afterthought, blurted out, "and I know the disco scene." This was partially true, since a mutual friend invited her to his restaurant opening, where she met Dr. Goshen, a dentist. He was immediately taken by Paula and had asked for her telephone number. After a few dates, she learned that he was into the disco scene, and loved going to Studio 54. He not only loved to dance, but enjoyed sniffing nitrous oxide—"sweet air," as she heard him call it. It gave him a buzz. Paula loved taking it all in, except for the oxide. His lifestyle was definitely not what a young widowed mother in the suburbs was seeking.

Who knows what combination of things worked in her favor with Mr. C? Her youth, her energy, her hope-hope-hope for the job, anything she said? All she remembered was within half an hour, he said, "You've got moxie, Paula. I like that. You look good, you speak up. I know this job isn't exactly up your alley, but if you're willing to work hard and put in long hours, I'll take the chance and hire you."

Paula lit up like a light bulb. And started to enthuse, "Oh thank . . . !"

He interrupted her with, "I'm glad to know this could be good for you. I need to make sure it's good for us. This is the hospitality industry. Do you know what that means?"

"Ye-es, Mr. C.," she stammered, hoping he wouldn't ask for a definition.

"The hours are long and you need to be thinking on the hotel's behalf all the time."

"I can do that," she said.

He reiterated that her responsibilities would include holiday functions, special events, and establishing a V.I.P. club membership for the cocktail lounge. "And I'll personally train you, Paula. I want to make this a success, since this is the first time we are hiring a PR person from within."

Her mouth was dry, and she remembered to take a breath. All she could think of was how important it would be to excel in this position. He was really going out on a limb hiring her—a never-before job by a never-before promotions person. "I'll make it work, Mr. C. I want this job and I know I can do it."

"Don't you want to know your compensation plan?" Her face turned crimson. How stupid could she be? He smiled broadly, saying, "You'll receive a weekly salary plus medical benefits for you and your son. The accounting office will call you to verify your package." Now she knew exactly how Cloud Nine felt. He stood up. "Welcome to the hospitality industry, Paula."

That night Paula invited her parents over for dinner. She splurged and served shrimp cocktail, porterhouse steak (her father's favorite cut of meat) and roasted herb potatoes. "It's a celebration!" she gleefully announced.

"Well, you can't have a celebration without wine and good food—*alla famiglia*," John raised his glass—to the family! That night, sleep came easily for Paula.

One week later, she reported to work. Mr. C was an exceptional mentor and teacher. The first day he spent an hour with her in his office explaining her duties. He showed her every nook and cranny of the hotel and reviewed all the details of the bar and restaurant, and clued her in as to who she could count on . . . or couldn't.

On the home front, Rose was caring for JB when he wasn't in school. Paula would generally get home by six p.m., prepare dinner, and review her son's homework with him. On many evenings, Rose would leave some food in the refrigerator for Paula to heat up. She enjoyed her work, but Mr. C was right. The hours were long. She felt guilty when her son called her at work, asking what time she would be coming home.

Within six months, her hard work started to pay off. She planned a Halloween extravaganza with a local radio station and arranged for a fog machine, a mirrored disco ball, and prizes for the most outlandish costumes. It was a huge success, and the party made the local newspapers, complete with a picture of one of the winning couples in nude body suits with strategically placed sequins. The next day, Mr. C called her into his office, a newspaper on his desk. She gulped, waiting for some shoe to drop. "Paula, we've never had publicity like this," he said. She was too scared to ask him if that was good or bad. "I'll tell you one thing," he continued, picking up a piece of paper with columns of numbers, "Drink sales were way up last night, so it was a big money maker for us."

"That's great!" she said, behaving as though he should be happy.

"Next time, do me a favor—clear what you're doing with me," he said, a hint of a smile appearing on his face. She left his office before it could be discussed further, thinking, at least the hotel got noticed. Isn't that what PR is all about?

More and more, the local papers would pick up stories about goings-on at the hotel. She was learning the importance of having a newsworthy event and good relationships with editors who were in a position to write about them. Every evening before departing for home she would check on the lounge activity. Since initiating a V.I.P. promotion in the cocktail lounge, the place was buzzing. The new alluring outfits the waitresses were now wearing certainly didn't hurt business. Executive types, lawyers, and brokers would frequently stop in after work for a cocktail.

Paula finest hour came when Jerry Anderson, an entertainment promoter, called her to book the Grand Ballroom for a live concert. "Who is the entertainer?" she asked.

"Peter Allen," he answered. Speechless, she repeated the performer's name.

She was well aware of this Australian talent, and replied, "Sure, why don't you come in and we can discuss this further."

Mr. C wasn't too familiar with Allen, but Paula knew that this was an incredible opportunity for the hotel. She told her boss they had to book this event. It would be big!

And it was. All the facilities were booked for the two shows; hotel rooms, the two restaurants and cocktail lounge. As she watched the young Peter Allen sing and dance to the tune "I Go to Rio," she felt a great sense of fulfillment. She loved this job!

Working long hours, she relished eating a family-style dinner at her folks' home every Sunday. During one such meal, her father suggested she start thinking of a permanent home to live with her son.

"What are you talking about, Dad? We have a permanent place."

"No, Honey, you have an apartment. You're paying rent every month. Have you considered buying a little place of your own?"

"OK, what do you have in mind for me?"

"I know a fellow who's developing a property with thirty townhouses. You should check them out," he suggested, saying, "Since they're condos, it would be easy for you to maintain." Knowing her father's thinking was usually right on target, she had to agree. She was gainfully employed, so she could qualify for a mortgage in her own name.

Why not, she thought. It would be reassuring to own property again, and besides, it would be a good investment for her. Things were definitely picking up.

Chapter 14

WORK–PLAY–
HEALTH

L IFE FOR PAULA HAD EASED INTO A ROUTINE of jug-
gling being a working girl and a mom. Within weeks
of starting her job, she realized that a position in the hotel
industry would also enable her to meet eligible men. After
several months of dating, she thought she was making some
progress with her dating skills, but apparently not her taste in
men. According to Rose and John, her dates were not passing
family muster. "Your taste in men is regressing," Rose said,
after meeting a couple of very acceptable fellows.

"What's the matter with Steven, Mom?" Paula asked.

"He looks like a marshmallow."

"Oh, he's just a little chubby."

"He looks like the Pillsbury Dough Boy," Rose countered.
For some reason Rose, the cooking aficionado that she was,
always found a way to equate men with everything from
soured milk to stale bread.

When her husband would overhear one of these exchanges,
John would add, "Your mother's right, Paula. Where are you

meeting these guys?" He'd say it with a bemused incredulousness, as though she had brought E.T. home.

While Paula pleaded ignorance, she understood what they were talking about. For instance, there was Neil, the businessman whose idea of paying her a compliment was, "Boy, you must have been beautiful when you were younger." She was now thirty-four.

Then there was the young man her father called Tiny Tim. He was short and wore elevated shoes, but made Paula laugh a lot. Even though he was the same age as she was, at times she thought his actions were very immature. No one could hold a candle to Tom.

While the men she dated quickly became the ongoing butt of family jokes at the dinner table, Rose asked one day, "Can't you meet an eligible man with character?"

She kept telling them what she knew to be true. "All the good guys are married. It's slim pickins out there."

In fact, it came to the point that she really didn't care much one way or another, since lately her best date was her hair dresser, Gary. When he needed an escort for weddings or bar mitzvahs, he would ask her (again, a good-looking Italian guy with great taste in clothes). He could dance, and to top it off, they both had moms with the same name, even born on the same day. It gave them a special bond. "How's your Rose?" he would ask.

"My Rose is fine. How's your Rose?" Paula would shout back, the two of them acting like teenagers who never stopped laughing at the same stupid joke. They got along so easily, they figured if they never met that special someone, they would end up living together. All Gary wanted was a young houseboy to take care of them in their old age. Paula agreed.

She could live with that. All Gary had to do was maintain her hair so she looked younger than her years.

About the same time, she became fast friends with one of her co-workers. They hit it off the first week she started working at the hotel. He welcomed her with genuine enthusiasm. "Aren't you cute?" he added, extending his hand. "I'm Joe Day."

"Joe Day, it's a pleasure to meet you," Paula said, finding herself smiling at his outgoing, cheerful manner. They enjoyed eating lunch together, and Joe supplied enough dish and gossip to keep her amused. She even got a kick out of his name, Joe Day, while he nicknamed her "Sunny Mooney." Joe hungered to be part of the "in" crowd in New York City with an eagerness approaching reverence. He loathed the term "wannabe." "I'm going to be!" he would insist, drawing up even taller than his six feet and sucking his stomach in.

Joe was a clean-cut, nice-looking twenty-four-year-old kid from Denville, New Jersey. Slightly pudgy, he worked in the accounting department. Like Batman, this burly suburban Irish kid by day was a starry–eyed big city player at night. At least three nights a week, he would drive into Manhattan in his little Honda Prelude, where he would party hearty. He seemed to know every DJ, bouncer, and bartender in the city and was a regular at Studio 54.

He had lots of friends, one of which was Elaine Steinbeck, widow of John Steinbeck. Actually, he was pals with Elaine's granddaughter, Andy, but Elaine found Joe entertaining. They would often share a Manhattan or Old-Fashioned cocktail together in her apartment on 72nd Street gossiping about who was cheating on whom, wearing what, going where, and having a high-society low-down good time. At lunch one day, Joe confided to Paula that he was envious of Elaine's lifestyle, and one day he would write his own book, and call it *Grapes of Envy*.

Between friends, work and family, life was satisfying for Paula. Before long, the days all blended into each other, and she welcomed the sameness of each day. She had enough roller-coastering to last her a lifetime. The predictability of her life was her new norm, until one particular day in May. She got to work later than usual, and Joey caught her on the way in, saying, "Paula, Mr. C's been looking for you. You better see what he wants." When she approached his open door, he gestured for her to come in and have a seat. Looking subdued, he hung up the telephone with a heavy hand.

"What's up, Mr. C?" she asked cheerily.

"Paula, I've been on the phone all morning with the corporate offices. I've just been informed that they're downsizing the advertising and promotional budget."

"What does that mean?" she asked, starting to feel queasy.

"It means your job is being terminated."

"You mean I'm fired?" she blurted out.

"No, you're not being fired—just your position. You can transfer to Catering Sales or any other department. I don't have a problem with your performance."

Paula was devastated. All she knew was that Mr. C created this position, and it was perfect for her. Pride got the best of her, because she heard herself saying she couldn't take Mr. C's alternate job offer at this time. She further rationalized her decision to walk would allow her more time to spend with her son, and deep down she had a guilty feeling that he needed her to be home.

When she told Joe what had happened, he said "Great, Sunny! Now we can work on a business plan of our own."

For months the two of them had talked about starting a business. They had previously chatted, nothing more serious than that, about how they each seemed to have great instincts for promotion. That seemed good enough for them to leap into the unknown. And that's what they did. Since Paula was now unemployed, why not start a little promotion and PR boutique? They called it Aware Concepts—"We make people aware that you're there," was the tag line.

Although they were both cockeyed optimists, Paula insisted that Joe keep his day job, just in case, while she went about trying to bring in accounts. It was a struggle, but since they delighted in each other's company, it was fun for a while. They landed several clients, but hardly enough to support one or even two people, so after a year they decided to call it quits.

Paula's father, now a youthful sixty-five-year-old, was retiring for the second time. His colleagues from the back office threw him a going-away party at a local tavern on Wall Street. Rather than letting her father take the train home on his last day of work, Paula along with her Mom drove from New Jersey to pick him up. John was in a jubilant mood that evening, so Paula insisted on their way home that they continue the celebration at Il Giordano's Restaurant, which was conveniently located outside the Lincoln Tunnel. It would be just the right spot for a nightcap with an entertainer she truly enjoyed.

A young Greek named Cosmos played the piano and guitar and sang international songs on a regular basis. Paula knew of this place from her time with Tom and their friends. After-dinner drinks were ordered, they sat in a living room–type atmosphere enjoying the lively music. Then a frisky John decided to dance like Anthony Quinn in *Zorba the Greek*.

Taking a white dinner napkin, he flipped it open and starting swaying his body to the music. Paula took hold of his other hand, and they both danced around the room. Rose, trying to be a good sport, yawned and smiled. All she really wanted to do was to curl up in the comfort of her own bed. By this time, she knew her husband was feeling the effects of the drinks—and the more he consumed, the more sentimental he became. Rose caught her daughter's eye, and with that one look, Paula knew it was time to go home.

Still in good health, John would now be collecting two pensions—one from the Postal Service and one from Morgan Stanley. The extra money would be used for travel and to help pay for JB's college education. It was a perfect plan. Or so he thought. "We plan, God laughs."

No sooner had John retired than Rose started to complain about her health. It came out of nowhere. All of a sudden, she had migratory pains, morning stiffness, chills, and fever. John's dreams of travel and especially of going to Italy to re-trace his roots were soon shelved. "On the back burner," he would optimistically say, certain that his wife's health issues would prove only temporary. Instead, he was spending more and more of his days taking Rose from one doctor to another to determine the cause of her illness. Finally, after numerous doctor visits and testing, she was diagnosed with polymyalgia rheumatica, an inflammatory disorder that causes widespread muscle aching and stiffness. She started taking Prednisone and found immediate relief, but her days were occupied with her poor health. Considering any trips abroad was out of the question.

"I'm not comfortable being out of the country, babe. What if I start feeling sick again?" John's crestfallen reaction led to some compromising. They decided to take some

Caribbean cruises, because then Rose wouldn't have to walk much. Frequent trips to Cape Cod to visit with cousins, and occasionally a flight to Florida to see Rose's brother Alex and his wife, Loly, were a welcomed relief for both of them.

As the next few years went by, John's dreams of travel abroad slipped away. Would he ever get to Italy? Paula was now concerned for both of her parents. Her mother's pain seemed to be getting worse. As a last resort they went to see the Chief of Rheumatology and Connective Tissue Disorders at St. Luke's Roosevelt Hospital in Manhattan. Every physician had a different opinion. They even questioned the diagnosis. She tried one drug after another—Penicillamine, Methotrexate, Voltarin, even Gold. Nothing seemed to ease the pain. It was rheumatoid arthritis, or, as one doctor suggested, "it could be the onset of something else."

They weren't quite sure the nature of this illness, because some days were better for Rose than others. When she was feeling up to it, she would spend hours by the stove and freeze the delicious foods her family enjoyed. When she was ill and bedridden, she gave her husband instructions on what to do and how to prepare the meals. John did the grocery shopping, kept the house in order, and tried to keep his wife's spirits up. At the same time, Rose encouraged her husband to invite his family over for dinner.

His nephew Tony lived less than an hour away and was a frequent visitor. His brother Ernie, whose beloved wife, Betty, had passed away from stomach cancer, was also a welcomed guest. He was bereft, as were their two adult daughters, who still lived at home in Staten Island. After about a year, Ernie started dating a lovely woman, a nurse, and his daughters behaved as though he had brought an ax murderer home. They treated her with enough iciness to fill the

Antarctic. Ernie no longer felt particularly comfortable in his own home, so he and his lady friend, Jean, were only too happy to accept John's invitation to come for dinner, spend the day, have a few pops, and forget everybody's troubles for a few hours.

Once in a while, John's sisters Tessie, Anna, and Catherine would visit, as well. This was a rarity, since none of them had ever learned to drive, and it meant a long round-trip train commute. But when they did venture outside of their boundaries for a day or two, it was sure to be a festive occasion. Whether it was cooking, cleaning anything they could get their hands on, or talking about old friends and family, the house would be filled with laughter. John was elated, and since he was the only alpha male among them, his sisters doted on him constantly. His sister, Anna, lost her husband, Vinny, early on. It was a stunning loss for her, since they were both in their fifties when a massive heart attack claimed him. As the years went by, Anna would complain about a lack of "Vitamin F." It took little imagination to know what four-letter word this 4'8" dynamo was talking about.

Similarly, Catherine reveled in making everybody laugh. Her husband had died, as well, apparently of alcohol-related liver failure. "Aaayyy, who needs to date anybody?" she would ask rhetorically. "I had enough of that little stick of Joe's to last me a lifetime. And, sonofabitch, was it little!" Tessie was the more restrained of the sisters. Her own marriage was a difficult one, but she endured.

During these family reunions, everyone delighted when they could share meals together. All of these women shared a similar bond. A homemade meal expressed their love for you! No one ever left their tables hungry, with antipastos fit for the finest restaurants, lamb roasts, pork loins, platters of veal scaloppini, stuffed *carciofi* (artichokes), and homemade manicotti filled with creamy ricotta cheese. Invited guest would invariably always bring desserts. Divine concoctions from the always-nearby Italian bakery, in large white boxes tied with string, in which you would find pastries like *sfogliatelli*, cannoli, Napoleons, or rum babas. "Who wants another cannoli?" "Wait, there's leftovers." "Take them home!" Italian, through and through.

Chapter 15

FAMILY SECRETS

I T's said that you can never truly know a per-son, who they really are, or what they really think. As close as the Maidas were as a family, this was even true of Rose and John. Paula thought she knew everything about her parents, including the fact that they were a study in contrasts—John was a jovial, diehard optimist. Even though he had his hands full taking care of Rose now, he'd use his trademark humor to add a smile whenever he could. "Paula," he'd say, "Mom is like a Timex watch, she keeps on tickin' even when she takes a lickin.'" He exuded warmth and playfulness, especially when sipping a glass of single malt Scotch. "I'm John Maida. I'm a happily married man. Just ask my mistress," he'd announce, gesturing toward Rose, who was clearly within earshot.

Rose, on the other hand, was a chronic worrier, constantly expressing fears and concerns for herself and her family. "Be careful, Paula, don't do that, it's too dangerous." "Are you sure you want to drive there? It's so far." "What if it doesn't work?" Half-full doesn't begin to describe her view of the world; possibly a quarter-full. Maybe hers was an inescapable sense of dread, given how unwanted she felt as a child. No matter how much good eventually came her way, she was always waiting for the next shoe to drop. More and more, she appeared resigned, morose. John did his best to lighten up those moods.

"Your family name, Marasco," he chided. "I bet it was really Morose. Your family must've changed their name when they got off the boat."

"Johnny, I know I married you for a reason, I just can't remember what it was," she'd say.

"Because my jokes are stupid and I love you, that's why," he'd answer.

No question, his cheerfulness was a stark contrast to his wife's. Those very differences help explain why they were drawn to each other. Apparently, opposites really do attract. Even as a child, Paula could feel the romantic energy that characterized their relationship. That remained a constant through their proverbial thick and thin.

Rose had her share of problems with in-laws, her parents, raising two daughters, and her own emotional state of being. In those early days, issues such as anxiety disorders were not topics of conversation. Any time a woman had problems, it was blamed on "the Change." Hormones gone haywire might well have played a part in Rose's medical issues as she got older, as she was certainly no stranger to panic attacks. On several occasions, when Paula was a young teen, her father would awaken her in the middle of the night and ask her to take care of her younger sister. John would then escort Rose to their family physician, who lived around the corner in a large, three-story brownstone; the medical office was in the basement with living quarters upstairs. Since John's brother Ernie was married to Dr. Barone's sister, Rose had access to medical care at all hours. All she had to do was put on her top coat over her nightgown.

Now approaching her mid-60s, Rose's body reflected its years of worry and anxiety. When John first met her, she was shapely and well-rounded. "Your mother had more curves than the Old Mill Road. She looked as good from the back as from the front," he mentioned with fond recollection. With each decade, she became thinner. By this time, she was almost bony and angular. Only her still-beautiful smile could erase the gauntness her face had taken on.

John, on the other hand, looked hale and healthy. The years had added a few jowls, along with some pounds that landed around his middle. But his sunshine personality never gave people the impression of anything but a man in the prime of his life. While Paula adored her dad, she valued her mother's sweetness, her love of fine things, her wanting only the best for her family. Whatever their innate differences, she took them at face value. They were who they were. Or were they?

The question came up out of the blue. Rose had gotten a call from her Aunt Regina in Brooklyn. "Oh, how sad. Where's the funeral going to be? When?" She explained the details as soon as she hung up the phone. Her Aunt Lena had passed away. The funeral Mass was being held at Regina Pacis Church in their old neighborhood in Brooklyn, a magnificent edifice that was built to honor Our Lady of Peace after a majority of the neighborhood boys came home safely from the war. Modeled after the domed churches of Italy, it was filled with marble, gilded ceilings, and magnificent stained glass.

Both Paula and her sister Marian attended Catholic School there and regularly attended nine a.m. Mass every Sunday (or else). It was in this church that many of the relatives were married and memorialized at death. There it was, a church built by immigrants, and its parishioners were very proud of its grandeur. John, once an usher there, even helped to raise funds for a new parochial school that the Monsignor wanted to build. This unexpected visit brought back many fond memories.

The day of the funeral, Paula decided to join her parents. The three of them ventured out that morning, Rose in her perennial black and white dress especially reserved for funerals and John in his seldom-worn dark gray suit. That day the church was filled with many relatives on Rose's side of the family, along with friends and neighbors paying their last respects to the deceased.

While John stopped to talk to an old friend, Rose and Paula sat in one of the impeccably varnished oak pews in the mid-section of the church. Within moments, Paula saw her mother's eyes widen as a nice-looking older man with silver hair passed their pew.

Rose seemed startled, and glanced around to see if anyone else was looking her way. Then she looked toward him again. Her face was ashen. "Mom, what's the matter, are you Okay? Who's that?" Paula asked. Then she noticed her father approaching.

"I'm all right, Paula," she answered. "I'll tell you later— Daddy's coming."

"What would she tell me?" Paula kept asking herself. When they drove back to New Jersey later that afternoon, John went out for Chinese food so Rose would not have to cook.

It had been a long day for all of them. With John out, Rose asked Paula to pour her a small cordial glass of Christian Brothers brandy. It was used for medicinal purposes in their home, and it helped to calm Rose's nerves.

"OK, Mom, what's this all about?" her daughter inquired. "You acted like you saw a ghost today."

"In a way, I did," she answered. "It's someone from a long time ago."

By now Paula's curiosity was off the charts. "Talk to me, Mom. I'm an adult now."

"Paula, when your father was stationed in England during the war, I met someone. He turned out to be a good friend."

"And was that him?"

She interjected. "Yes, that was Ralph."

"No shit. That was an old boyfriend?"

"Paula, don't talk like that, it's so crude."

"Sorry, it's just such a surprise. Tell me more."

"No, I think that's quite enough for now, and Daddy will be back soon."

She did tell Paula more. In fact, she seemed eager to reveal, at long last, the secret that had gnawed at her for so many years. Over the next few weeks she confided the whole story to her eldest daughter. She had met Ralph through friends of her family. It was an all-too-familiar tale during the war years. Rose was lonely. Ralph was older and handsome and they spent many hours together. The biggest surprise of all was when she told her daughter that she had become pregnant and had an abortion. It was a male fetus.

"Did Dad know about this?" Paula asked, careening between tenderness and incredulity.

"No, never. He suspects there might have been someone when he was overseas, but he doesn't know."

"That's good, Mom, it's your life." She had no difficulty talking to her mother as a girlfriend, rather than a daughter. She instinctively knew it was important that she treat her mother and this secret with respect.

"Mom, it was a different time and place, I understand." Paula was being honest, she did understand. Her mother's single indiscretion might seem like a joke in this day and age, but that was not the case then. Rose was relieved to finally be able to talk about it, though she clearly felt a lot of guilt. Paula felt honored that her mother had taken her into her confidence, and the bonds between mother and daughter strengthened that day.

But at the same time, she could see how much her mother was suffering from physical pain. It was obvious that her pain was increasing. It showed in her eyes and in her achingly slowed mobility. Rheumatoid arthritis was taking its toll. This disease was sapping her energy as her own immune system was eating away at healthy joint tissue and bone. The long-term use of corticosteroids could suppress the immune system for a time, but only with the cost of terrible side effects. Once, Rose was a pretty and vivacious woman. She felt desire and passion. Today, she was frail and tired.

Infidelity had haunted her and now, forty years later, she could talk to her own daughter about it. Both mother and daughter also knew that this was a secret they could never share with the man they both loved. John didn't need to be hurt that way—there was no reason to divulge this news. It served no purpose.

Chapter 16

IN YOUR FACE

"Hey, MARIAN, I was just making some coffee."

"Gotta go, Mom! Grandpa's giving me a driving lesson."

"Paula, we're going to Shop Rite. Do you need anything?"

"Yeah, get some fish for tonight. Ask Pat what's fresh today."

The family moved to and from each other's homes as though they were one. In fact, they all had keys to each other's front doors. A few minutes apart, a short drive away, is all the distance they required for privacy—no boundaries existed. Call it family craziness, but it worked for them.

Eventually, Marian and Wayne moved to New Jersey. Other men would have balked at commuting an extra hour to go to work to be near their in-laws, but not Wayne. He was of Norwegian and Scottish descent, a strapping fellow of 6'2"with a bushy head of blonde hair and strong hands. Marian was all of 5'4"and as Italian looking as her older sister. With almond-shaped eyes and dark, thick curly hair, she was forever watching what she ate to keep her figure in check. Both girls definitely looked liked sisters—at times people would ask if they were twins. This comment totally infuriated Marian, since she was several years younger of the two. It didn't take much convincing for Wayne to agree that moving was a good idea. A blue collar worker in the plumbers' union, he worked for the New York City Board of Education. His spare time was spent boating and fishing. He was a likeable guy through and through, a very decent man with a kind heart.

It was obvious to Rose that her son-in-law, Wayne, wasn't raised in a loving and warm environment. He hardly talked about his parents—his mother was very detached emotionally and remote. This could well explain Wayne's caring nature when he was in the company of Rose. He appreciated the passion that she put into her cooking, especially since his wife was just the opposite. They would often have conversations about food or his catch of the day. "Your mother is the only person who understands me," he would often tell his wife.

Yes, Rose understood all too well how lack of affection and criticism could pierce a person's spirit. Wayne would do anything for Rose if she asked him. John couldn't have been more pleased about the impending move. "Marian, it's about time you and Wayne start a family. JB's been my only grandchild for 16 years!" he said. "Maybe he isn't lonely, but I am!"

"Yeah, Marian," Paula chimed in.

"Given my current prospects of no one, the Widow Mooney is not likely to have another baby." Paula was still doing the dating scene, but most of the men she was meeting all seemed to have issues. Immaturity, ex-wives, impotence, you name it. Was this mediocrity at its best? Weren't there any decent men around who wanted a normal relationship with a woman? The few men she did like made it known immediately that they had no intentions of remarrying and adding to their alimony woes. Dinner and sex were all that they wanted.

Both the girls knew it was getting more and more difficult for their parents at home. Having Marian nearer would be a big help to John. It would offer him some relief so he could go shopping, take a walk, or even take a needed afternoon nap, for that matter. Paula was concerned for her father. His main function now was being his wife's caretaker. Although John was never one to complain, his sense of humor could only keep him afloat for so long.

Moreover, Marian and her Mom always had a special bond. They would hang out together and play "Girlfriends," a game Marian devised when she was seven. "Mommy, let's play girlfriends," she'd say, "I'll be Angie." Then Marian would dress up, wearing lipstick, jewelry, and an old hand-bag that her Mother no longer used, which Marian filled with make-up, trinkets, and a couple of dollars. "Mommy says you should never leave the house without some money. You never know if you'll need it to get home." Decades later with her Mother's deteriorating health, this little charade was played out once again. Marian would fuss with Rose's hair, polish her nails, make her tea, and they would sit and watch the soaps together. Late in the afternoon, she would go home to get supper ready for Wayne.

With Marian living so close, John did the grocery shopping for all of his family if they asked him. It got him out of the house, and he could chat with the store owners and merchants in town. Rose taught him how to select produce and fruits, and now she was giving him cooking lessons. Under her tutelage, he was becoming quite an accomplished cook. He could bread and fry cutlets, make a zesty tomato sauce, and he could even add making meatballs to his repertoire. He added a secret ingredient to his wife's meatball recipe, which he refused to reveal to anyone. Whenever John was in the kitchen frying meatballs, Paula and JB would sneak eating one or two hot out of the frying pan. Rose would catch this action from the corner of her eye and reprimand the two of them. "Stop eating the meatballs. They're for the gravy."

Each family member was cast in a role. Always in each other's places and faces, they thrived in this relationship. Pity the outsider! The word dysfunctional wasn't known to them. Too close? Too needy? To them, they were a typical family. John's mother, Angelina, understood these things and would have been pleased . . . the ties that bind a family together are distinctively idiosyncratic.

Chapter 17

MR. ELUSIVE

"Paula, I decided to buy some phone company stock for you," John announced one day.

"Great! Fine, Dad." He could have bought her green cheese from the moon for all she cared. Her father was pretty good at picking stocks and watching the family's finances.

"We'll see you later. Remember, Uncle Alex and Aunt Loly are coming for dinner."

"I know, Dad. And they haven't seen JB in a long time, so I'll make sure my son makes an appearance," she said, mimicking the instructions John had given her a few days earlier.

Her father smiled, as though she had just said the smartest thing he'd ever heard. "See ya later, smartie pants." Even with all his wife's medical issues, he seemed content. He was happy to have his family around him, and that's all that seemed to matter.

Paula was now feeling as though she finally had been free of the weight of widowhood. The dark cloud was lifting with each passing day. With her father managing the money from Tom's small insurance policy and her Social Security payments, Paula was financially okay for the present. She was breathing easier these days and enjoyed condo living. Plus the freedom of not working at the hotel anymore gave her time to volunteer on the condominium board.

It wasn't very long before her skills were noticed and the president of the homeowners association asked her if she would consider becoming the manager. "Paula, you always seem to be the one to initiate the projects we need taken care of. We know you have a good eye for details. We can't pay much, but it's something." Paula was thrilled with this opportunity. If anything, she was overly concerned with paint chipping on exterior walls, how the lawns looked, and the overall appearance of the place. These were details she had gotten used to when she owned her own home.

Her Aunt Catherine had a different idea. "We're crazy, Paula. Some people paint. Some people make a ton of money. Italian women, we clean and cook." Even Paula's friend Gary reinforced that sentiment, joking "Italian women are born with a rag in their hand."

Now that she was comfortably ensconced in her new abode, spontaneous gatherings were commonplace. Friday night get-togethers had become a TGIF routine with her friends: Phyllis, Dee Dee (both in real estate, divorced, and wickedly funny), Joe, and Gary. Gary had a new boyfriend, Charles Coffey III. "Gary, wherever did you meet such a sweet man," Paula asked.

"Honey, do you mean Chuckles? Don't ask! More details than a straight woman needs to know. But he's a keeper, this one, and I mean for him to keep me in style."

Occasionally, her teenage son, JB, would come up from the finished basement. He had his own little man cave down there—television, stereo, and his musical equipment. His mom would frequently request that he play a tune on the piano for her friends. The group would then shoot the breeze, drink jug wine, and relax in each other's company with take-out pizza or Chinese. Or, if Paula was so inclined, cook a simple meal.

At the end of the evening, Gary would always ask for something sweet to eat. "Paula, any chocolate in the house?"

"You have the munchies, Gary?" Dee Dee would ask.

"And you told us those were only Marlboros you were smoking," Phyllis would chime in.

"Smart asses, what's for dessert?" he'd ask again.

"How about some Oreo cookies and a glass of milk?" Paula chimed in.

"Who do you think I am, your son?"

"I wish! Look at all the money I'd save on haircuts and blow dries. Okay, I'll get the ice cream."

Paula was adjusting to single life in the suburbs. Being a married woman was off her agenda, especially now that she realized many people were divorced these days. The family humorist, Aunt Catherine, concurred. "Being single is really nice, Paula. You do what you want. Fart when you want. Like the trees in the forest, ya know? No one's around to hear it." Paula had to agree with her. Life was simple and she was in control. Or so she thought!

Later that year, a new resident moved into the complex where she was living. The owner of a unit decided to lease out his property for investment income. Paula had seen the paperwork about his tenancy and had to send him the usual forms about association rules. All she knew was his name, Richard Madden, and that he was listed as the sole tenant on the lease. JB was the first to notice him. Actually he noticed the cars he was driving. "Hey, Mom, do you see all the great cars that guy has? A white Porsche, a BMW, and a 450 SEL Mercedes."

"Yes, I saw that. I might have to talk to him about that, since the by-laws only allow one car in the garage and one parking place per unit."

"Mom, don't break his *cajones*."

"JB! Where do you learn things like that?"

What had really caught her attention were not the cars but the man behind the wheel. She definitely found his looks appealing. He wasn't classically handsome, but he had the rugged good looks of a man's man, well-built with large, broad shoulders, over six feet tall, and trim. When she saw him coming and going in his golf or running clothes, it was easy to see that he had an athletic physique. Yes, she most definitely had noticed this guy. She figured he was in his forties—Paula seemed to be attracted to older and tall men. Her son's comments about all the cars he was driving piqued her own interest further. What better way to gather information than to send her son on a fact-finding mission? "JB, find out anything you can about him for me. This could be fun."

"Why, Mom, you interested or something?"

"Well, you never know; maybe he's a car dealer, a good connection, don't you think?"

"Sure thing, Mom, will do."

A few Saturdays had passed when JB noticed two little girls playing soccer outside of Mr. Madden's unit. That's when he hit pay dirt. He went outside and started talking to them. "OK, Mom, here's the story. The girls are named Mara and Anny. He's in the process of getting a divorce. The girls are his daughters. They see their father on weekends when he's in town, and heck, he's in the sporting goods industry, not cars."

"Oh, so he travels a lot, but why so many cars?"

"I think he just likes cars, Mom."

Months went by, and one day while Paula was parking her own car, the UPS man tried to deliver a package to Mr. Madden. "I guess he's not home, Tommy," she commented. "He travels a lot, I hear." Knowing that she was the manager, Tommy asked if she would sign for the package. Frequently doing this for owners, accepting packages, mail, newspapers, special deliveries, she did. "No problem, Tommy. I'll take the package and notify him when he returns."

"Thanks, Ms. Mooney."

This was perfect. Paula now had an opportunity to meet the infamous Richard Madden face to face. She left a note in his mailbox that she had accepted a package for him, and to please contact her to pick it up, very clearly writing her telephone number down. A week later he called. "Hi, this is Rich Madden. Thanks for taking that package for me. Can I come over now to pick it up?" he inquired.

"Well, I'm just on my way out the door, Mr. Madden. I can bring it over to you now?"

"That would be great, I'll meet you at the front door," he said. Paula was heading out to meet a friend for lunch; she grabbed the package and took a quick look in the mirror to make sure she looked presentable. With her car keys and package in hand, she quickly walked to his unit.

"Thanks so much," he said, taking the package from her. "I just returned from Europe, and I appreciate this," his eyes giving her the once over. "By the way, what size are you?"

"Excuse me," she said, thinking, "What kind of a question is that?" He must have noticed the surprised look on her face and quickly added, "Oh no, I was just asking because

I'm CEO of Adidas USA and I think you would look great in a warm-up suit."

"Oh, that's not necessary, Mr. Madden."

"No, please call me Rich, not Dick but Rich. You look like a size six? Let me get you a ladies' small. I insist." As she waited in his foyer, he went upstairs to get her a suit. Looking around the living room, she observed that it was simple but tastefully decorated. At least he's neat, she said to herself.

When he came down the stairs and he handed her a white warm-up suit, she said, "Really Rich, this is not necessary. I'm the manager, it's my job." But she smiled a big smile, since she was delighted by his gesture, and the fact that he got her size right. "Thank you so much. Gotta run, I'm late for a lunch date." A serendipitous encounter with UPS just landed her a warm-up suit and an introduction to Rich Madden. In those brief minutes she could tell that he had a big personality, and a bigger opinion of himself. It sure didn't take him long to let her know he was a CEO. She couldn't blame him. Why shouldn't he be proud of that?

Her stomach had a queasy feeling; she was attracted to this man. Carefully, she had to calculate her next step. Paula decided a nice thank you note was in order for the athletic suit. It read, "Nice to meet you, Rich, sorry I had to rush out, please come over for a cocktail when you have the time so we can chat further." Thinking she was very clever, he never called. It wasn't until a year later that they met again. While she was walking in the local park, he was running in the other direction. "Hi, Paula," he said, and stopped running.

"Hi, Rich," she said, acting totally nonchalant and indifferent. "How are you?"

"Oh, travel too much these days. Haven't you noticed I'm never around?"

"Really, must be tough," she offered.

Suddenly he smiled. "Hey, do you have any plans this weekend? How about dinner with me?"

"This weekend?" she asked in return. "Uh, it's possible . . . I don't know. Let me check my schedule. My number is in the book. Give me a call," she suggested, knowing she would feel better if his offer were less than completely impromptu. She honestly didn't give it another thought. With him, it could be another year. That same evening he called, saying it was his younger daughter's birthday on Friday, and he was taking a group of little girls out to celebrate. Was she free on Saturday night? "Saturday night? Well, I might be," she said, with some hesitation.

Maybe it was just the games people play. But women were always taught as young girls never to seem too eager. He ignored her game-playing completely. "Great, pick you up at 7:30."

She surprised herself when she added, "Why not come over at seven, and we can have a cocktail before dinner?"

"Super, see you then. Looking forward to it, Paula."

As Paula hung up the receiver, it dawned upon her that, finally, after almost two years, she had just landed a dinner date with Mr. Elusive. Once again, she had that funny feeling in her stomach. All day Saturday she felt anxious in a good way. First dates can be a disaster, so-so, or knock-your-socks off fabulous. "JB, what should I wear tonight?"

"Oh, Mom, you always look good."

"No, really, help me out here. What do you think? I value your opinion." The fact was she did. Her son had a great sense of style. Maybe it was having so many adults around him, but he had a budding sophistication that was becoming increasingly apparent.

"You have pretty legs, Mom. Wear a skirt." Sonofagun, if he wasn't gonna be a lady killer.

"Thanks, sweetheart. I'll wear my gray wool skirt, silk blouse and pink jacket." All of a sudden, she said, "But wait a minute, suppose he comes casual?"

"Mom, this guy looks like as class act. Don't worry, he will wear a jacket."

The doorbell rang. Her heart was pounding as her hand turned the brass knob to the left, and she opened the door. With his swaggering good looks, Rich Madden was standing there looking pretty dashing himself. He was wearing a navy double-breasted jacket, tie, white/cranberry striped shirt, and gray slacks.

Bearing a bottle in hand, he said, "Paula, I thought you might like champagne for an aperitif. Nicholas Feuillatte, it's one of my favorites."

"Lovely, Richard, just lovely. I adore champagne." She escorted him into the living room and then to the kitchen so he could open the bottle for them. He looked around approvingly.

"Your home is very attractive, Paula, like you." While she reached for the champagne glasses, she noticed his French cuff shirt with his monogram on the sleeve, RJM, and gold cufflinks. Her son was right. This guy was a class act.

A little voice inside her kept saying, "Be careful, Paula. It also echoed, 'Let the games begin.'"

Chapter 18

LOVE OR LUST

F IRST DATES CAN SEEM TERRIBLY AWKWARD, but
that evening felt different right from the beginning for
Paula. Richard had made reservations at a cozy restaurant
in the country. He gallantly opened the car door for her,
saying, "Buckle up, Paula, you're precious cargo to me." That
was a line she had never heard before. Dinner was followed
by slow dancing at a cocktail lounge closer to home, where
he then proceeded to tell her that he had his eyes on her for
a very long time.

"Oh, really, why the hesitation? If you recall, I did invite
you over for a cocktail a while back."

"Life has been so chaotic for me lately, Paula, and I saw
you had a boyfriend."

"Me, have a boyfriend?" She was dating, but she didn't
have anyone special in her life.

"Yes, the guy with the glasses, he comes to visit you a lot."

"You mean my father?" she laughed.

"That's your father?"

"Well, Richard if he's wearing glasses, dark complexion,
has a great smile, and a key to my place, that's My Johnny—my

Dad." They both found that amusing and continued to talk. As the evening progressed, the hours seemed to rush by too quickly; Paula didn't want the evening to end. She invited Richard back to her place for a cup of espresso. By sheer coincidence, JB had been invited to a friend's home for a sleepover that night. Paula thought of that fact when she extended the invite for coffee.

Oh heck, she thought, he will probably think I planned this all along. As they sat in the living room sipping coffee, she started a fire in the fireplace to ease the chill of the late hours. Like two souls that were destined to find each other, they talked throughout the night. There was so much to discuss. Richard was an intelligent and highly complex man with an interesting past.

He grew up in Queens, New York. Parents married when they were in their mid-thirties. An Irish father (a stern and devout Catholic) with a strong work ethic married a woman whose father was born in Germany. She was an accomplished organist and they met in the church choir. Richard had four siblings, three brothers and one sister. His sister passed away at eighteen from cystic fibrosis. When the kids were still young, the family moved to Connecticut. In keeping with their parents' belief that idle hands were the devil's work, all the sons had jobs early on to help support themselves. Richard had several jobs in his youth: paper boy, caddie, and dishwasher at a local country club.

Leaving home right after high school to attend the United States Naval Academy, he married his high school sweetheart upon graduation. He had two sons and earned an MBA from Harvard. Before she could ask a question, he said, "The relationship was doomed to fail. We were so young when we married. What did we know about life or what we wanted? Heck, we were just two Irish kids with parents who were too strict. We were both happy to get the hell out of our homes. The boys are both in college now."

"You have two sons, Richard," Paula interjected. "What about your daughters?"

"My second marriage," he answered. "I met my second wife when I was working in California; in fact it was at a Catholic retreat."

Second wife? Jeez, how many are there?, she thought.

He didn't pick up on her discomfort and proceeded to tell her how different his second wife was from his first. "She was brilliant, but the relationship had its challenges." Paula was beginning to deflate faster than a flat tire.

She sounds perfect, plus gives him two children. What does it take to keep this guy happy? He seemed to understand where her mind was going, and quickly stopped extolling her virtues and said, "Some years later, she was diagnosed as manic-depressive." Paula knew that shouldn't have made her feel better. But it did. "It was a roller-coaster ride for me," he said, his face showing the difficulties he'd had coming to terms living with a woman who was high, low, and nowhere in-between.

"I wanted the marriage to work out for the girls' sake, but eventually she was the one who wanted out. I hired a competent South American woman to live-in, cook, clean and watch over the girls when they're not in school."

Even his professional life was fraught with complexities. He recounted his background, and Paula was beginning to feel more and more as she felt when she had first met Tom. Richard told her he'd worked for several companies in the automotive industry and then went on to acquire the exclusive distribution rights for Kleber Tires in North America. He developed such a lucrative foothold in the states that Michelin France, which had later bought Kleber France, wanted to reclaim the distribution from him. They were pressuring him to sell his company back to them. "I hate the stronghold they have me in. I'm damned if I do, damned if I don't."

Apparently his reputation had become known in a lot of corporate circles, because in addition to his distributorship, he'd been recruited and hired by Kaethe Dassler, the matriarch of Adidas in Germany to become its first chief executive officer in the United States.

"My white warm-up suit," Paula chimed in.

"Exactly." He smiled. Then his face took on a pained expression. "I enjoyed that job, but I've been through the wringer." He went on to explain that his position was jeopardized from the start by the Dassler family's only son, Horst. "He gave me a difficult time from the start because his mother went outside the family to give me the CEO position in America. Bottom line, he was a control freak, and he was named president of Adidas a year before his mother's death. Eventually he terminated my employment," he said quietly.

"You mean you're not working now? Oh, Richard, how awful."

"Yes, it's certainly been that. I know it sounds like sour grapes, Paula, but I was too far ahead in my thinking for that company. I wanted to take Adidas public and buy back distribution. Horst favored the idea, but apparently did not want the scrutiny of public disclosure. He was advised by a conservative CFO in Germany that this plan was too radical a move. I wanted Adidas to better compete with Nike, but they would not hear of it. But let me tell you what they did want." He stopped long enough to take a sip of the cognac he'd been nursing. She couldn't wait to hear what he had to say next. "They asked me to deliver two million dollars in cash for under-the-table payments to athletes during the 1984 Los Angeles Olympics. Their way was the only way. I refused to do it."

"Maybe they were looking for any excuse to fire you," she said, questioningly.

"I'll admit that I'm not a very diplomatic type of guy, but I'll be damned if I was going to do something that was illegal. In the end I was terminated just before the summer Olympics." Then his face brightened as he jokingly added, "That sour kraut's ego was bigger than his Davidoff cigar."

Listening very attentively to every word he was saying, Paula couldn't help but think that her life was a piece of cake by comparison. Sure, she had personal losses, but her life seemed less unhinged and more grounded. She truly felt sorry for him as he spoke. He seemed lost at this time of his life, and again she felt grateful for her support system. She found herself wondering if her parents would approve of Richard Madden.

"My God, Paula it's three o'clock in the morning!" Richard said with complete astonishment.

She was surprised as he was. "Where did the night go?" she asked.

"Well, it's a lot closer to morning now. I'm so sorry . . ."

"Don't even think of apologizing," she said sincerely and meant it. "I've had a wonderful time."

They both stood up, and Richard gently tilted her face toward his, "You are one beautiful woman, Paula Mooney." And he kissed her ever so gently.

"Can this beautiful woman make you some breakfast?" she asked, feeling like she wanted to talk to this guy forever. She no sooner said it, then yawned. He laughed.

"Tell you what; I'm going to grab some shut-eye. You do the same. What time shall I come back for breakfast?"

"How's nine o'clock? Are you sure that isn't too early for you?" Paula knew she would never be able to fall asleep. She was feeling a happy thrill at getting to know him.

"No, that'll be fine.

"Come hungry."

"That's never a problem," he answered.

She wasn't fully sure it was still breakfast he was talking about. He came back at nine sharp, looking freshly showered and shaved, wearing a comfortable sweat suit. For whatever reason, they were both ravenous. Paula prepared a big Sunday morning breakfast of pancakes, scrambled eggs, and bacon.

Who should leisurely saunter in at ten o'clock but her father. "Hey, smells good in here." He was surprised to see his daughter wasn't alone. "Hi sweetheart, I was just on my way to the bakery to buy crumb buns for mom," he said, looking squarely at Richard, though addressing her.

As she was about to introduce them to each other, Richard stood up straight as if at attention, an old navy habit she gathered, and put out his hand to her father. "Sir, glad to meet you."

"Hiya, Richard. Enjoy your, uh, breakfast," John said a bit feebly, unsure of the breakfast for two he'd just interrupted. He got out of there fast, giving Paula the high sign to call him.

Paula knew he would tell his wife the minute he got home, and she would have some explaining to do about a guy in her kitchen on a Sunday morning. Sure, she was thirty-eight years old, but she still felt like she owed her parents an explanation. It didn't matter. She thought Richard Madden was the best thing that had happened to her since Tom. Except here, there'd be no subterfuge. So he was still married. He was legally separated. So he had kids. Hey, this was the 1980s!

Richard and Paula were inseparable from that day on. Two weeks later he invited her to his Harvard Reunion weekend. She later found that he had originally extended the invitation to someone else who he had dumped for Paula. Good thing she didn't know that then, because she didn't like men who did that sort of thing. On the drive up to Harvard, Richard insisted they stop off to visit his two younger brothers and their families in Connecticut. Showing me off, she suspected. Later on in the car he said, "Paula, I'm going to make you fall in love with me." She didn't want to tell him, but she had strong feelings for him already.

Rose thought her daughter was crazy. "Paula, from what you tell me about this man, he has a lot of baggage. Do you know what you are doing getting involved with Richard? Two marriages. Two sets of children."

John had to agree with his wife on this one. "How old is he?" he asked suspiciously. "He's forty-seven," Paula answered. "He's been around a lot of blocks," John answered disapprovingly.

"Oh, stop it," she said laughing. "He's only nine years older than I."

John looked dejected. "I forgot you're not a kid."

"I'll always be your little girl," Paula said, adding, "And you'll always be my Johnny." He gave Paula one of his sheepish ardent looks, his deep-set brown eyes so demonstrative.

"Honey, just be careful that's all, take it slow."

"Sure, Dad, I know you and Mom are just looking out for me." But Paula knew she was just giving her parents lip service. She was having too much fun with Richard, and their sexual attraction for each other was insatiable.

In early June, Richard introduced Paula to his daughters. Two very athletic little girls of nine and eleven; easy to be with, they seemed to enjoy JB's company. This made going out as a group more like a family. Like many couples in the early throes of a romance, they had names for each other. Richard was "Huggy Bear," Paula was "Honey Bear," and they called the children "Honey Cubs."

Silly as it sounds, it made them feel like they were connecting. Later that summer the girls went with their mother to visit their grandmother in Los Angeles. JB was scheduled to go to music camp that month. Richard announced that he had to go to Paris. He was being forced to sell his company back to Michelin and had to negotiate the deal. "Paula, would you like to accompany me to Paris? We could have fun together after my meetings are over."

"Would I? Are you crazy, Richard? Of course I would." She gave him a big hug.

Paris, the city of lights . . . they stayed at the Hotel Lancaster on the Right Bank. Paula explored the city while Richard and his attorney were in negotiations. During late evening suppers, they indulged their palates at fine restaurants (Julia Child would be so proud of me, she thought), consuming extraordinary wines. One of her favorite places to dine was Le Coupe Chou, near the Sorbonne. It was utterly romantic; rooms filled with antiques, walls made of stone, candlelight, and Vivaldi music playing in the background.

After the negotiations were over, they toured the wine country and the surrounding area of Beaune. By complete accident they came upon intimate lodgings at the Hotel De La Poste. Informed by the matron at the front desk that there was just one room left, they were escorted to view it. It was utterly charming, to Paula's delight—fireplace, big brass bed, and lots of antiques. The room rate included a gourmet four-course supper, which included local pastries and cheeses for dessert. Since Beaune is the principal center of the Burgundy wine trade, they sampled local estate bottles at every meal. It was in Beaune that Paula acquired a taste for Kir Royale, a small portion of blackberry liqueur topped with champagne, as a pre-dinner cocktail. This so-called business trip felt more like a honeymoon to her. Afterwards, they would retreat to their hotel room and end the evening with romance. It felt utterly divine and decadent.

Upon their return to the states, Paula's parents were hyper-inquisitive about this Paris holiday, or "fling," as they liked to refer to it. Making sure to spare her parents all of the details, Paula enthusiastically detailed her trip with Richard. "Oh, Daddy, Paris is such a beautiful city—the lights, the wine, especially the champagne. I'm going to marry Richard," she blurted out loud.

"Paula, I think you have champagne bubbles in your think tank these days. Slow down, Honey."

"Dad, don't be annoyed with me. It just feels so right when I'm with him. He needs me."

"Yes, honey, I know the two of you have goo-goo eyes for each other, but you hardly know him. It's only been four months." Again, he was cautioning her.

Was she being too impulsive these days? Were her parents right? For a brief few seconds, she pondered her own questions. Nope, she didn't think so. She reassured herself that her instincts with Richard were right on. "I just need to spend more time with my family to mollify the situation and diffuse their concern. Just act normal." She repeated this over and over.

Chapter 19

COME SEPTEMBER

"HI HONEY . . . GEE, ITS NINE O'CLOCK. You're just getting up?"

"Oh hi, Dad. Uh, late night . . ."

"Yeah, I bet it was! Mom is making her famous angel food cake. How's around six?"

"Oh Dad, I'd love to, but Richard and I have plans this evening."

"Well, how about this weekend, we'd like to take all the family out to dinner?"

"Dad, I'm so sorry, but this weekend Richard is taking me to his Naval Academy reunion."

"Hell Paula! Doesn't Richard ever stay home?" her father exploded one day.

Paula was feeling guilty, happy, and satisfied at the same time. She really was trying to allocate more time to her family, but Richard required so much of her attention.

"Hey, lady, did anyone ever tell you that you have a great body?"

"Huggy Bear, do you say that to all the women whose breasts you're nibbling?" Paula coyly replied.

"No, only to one beautiful Italian brunette who excites me just to look at her body."

Paula loved playing games with him; he made her feel so womanly and sexy. Honestly, she couldn't recall Tom making her feel that way; it was over seven years now since his death. All Paula had left were photographs to remind her of their life together, and one talented son who underestimated his ability. He was spreading his wings these days, and that concerned her.

It finally became apparent to both Paula and Richard that their ebullient behavior over the summer had to slow down. September was right around the corner, and the children would be going back to school in less than one week. They both had responsibilities and work to accomplish. Paula saw first hand that Richard was a caring father and an excellent provider for his family. And he was genuinely interested in their daily life, especially when it came to sports. Like many men, Richard was a lunatic at the girls' soccer games. Since Paula never really got into sports, she decided she could teach the girls other things; specifically, how to dress like girls. They were tomboys through and through, albeit pretty ones at that. She especially got a kick watching the youngest one play. Anny had a killer instinct on the soccer field. With her cute pixie haircut, she looked like an angel but played aggressively.

"Dad, how about if I invite Richard's daughters to dinner at your house?"

"That's very sweet, Paula. Let's just give it a while, okay?"

Paula's life was becoming a little schizoid: trying to be the good daughter, watching over her own son, and now trying to get to know Richard's girls. When she mentioned this to her sister one day, Marian erupted. "Oh, poor Paula. Nobody sees you anymore, and we're not happy that you have all these people to worry about." It didn't seem like a good time to mention her demands as property manager. With winter approaching, she had to get estimates for snow removal, review the operational budget, and oversee any work that needed to be done on the property.

"Honey Bear, I think I'm onto a good lead."

"Richard, that's wonderful. Wanna tell me about it?"

"When and if I clinch it, we'll celebrate." He was looking into starting a new business. He wanted to expedite his long-term goal, which was to retire early so he could play golf as often as he liked, and be captain of his own destiny. In many ways Richard reminded Paula more and more of her late husband. Both men were highly competitive, enjoyed golf, liked to have their evening cocktails, and both were smart, savvy businessmen.

Even their ethnic background was the same—Irish father, German mother. One thing that Richard excelled at that Tom lacked was his skill to remember things. Total recall; if you told him something once, it was imprinted in his mind. Paula often told Richard he should have become a trial attorney, with his uncanny ability to remember facts and dates. She was also learning to be careful what she told him in conversation, knowing that someday this talent may come back to hurt her. Men were funny that way, she had learned, especially if they had a few libations in them.

Paula made it a point to stop over to see her folks frequently these days. Her visits often caught her father tending to the lawn or cooking. In the kitchen one day, while chopping onions to put in a beef stew, the conversation came around to Richard again. "Honey, I know you are nuts about him, but why does a guy end up with two divorces, kids all the hell over the place?" her father asked.

"Give him a chance, Daddy. He's really smart and sweet and . . ."

"Yeah, yeah, I know. Love is blind."

"Dad! I know Richard very well."

"Oh right. It's been, what now, six months?"

Paula surmised her parents had way too much time to dwell on things. She, on the other hand, had other things to think about. Her son was turning sixteen soon and was going a hundred miles an hour.

"Mom, I got my driving permit! Mom, I'm forming a rock band! Mom, I'll be on the debating team this semester! Mom, Richard says when I get my license he'll let me drive his Mercedes around the school! Mom, uh, Susan asked me to the junior prom next month." JB took to girls as naturally as a fish to water. He was charming and made them feel special. She could already see trouble ahead.

"Be a gentleman. You know what I'm talking about," she constantly reminded him.

That fall, the leaves on the trees were turning a magnificent shade of orange, red, and gold. With the sun shining brightly into the Maida dining room, the family gathered around the table to enjoy a typical Sunday dinner that consisted of salad, pasta, and a meat course. Suddenly the telephone rang.

John answered, "Hi Tess . . . oh, oh Tess . . . oh, I'm so sorry. When did he die?" They all stopped whatever they were doing to listen. "Now what?" When John hung up, he said, "My sister's pretty shook up. Andy died. She kept saying they almost made it to their fiftieth anniversary."

"Johnny, what funeral home will he be laid out at?" Rose asked, as if she didn't know already.

John replied, "I told Tessie I'd call Eddie. He'll handle everything. I told her to pick out a nice suit for Andy to wear." John hung his head, looking forlorn. "My poor sister. Andy was sick for so long. She took care of him like a baby."

"Maybe it's better, Dad," Paula said. "How old is Aunt Tessie now?"

Rose answered, "She's 72, maybe 73."

Marian seemed to read her sister's mind. "Well, maybe she'll have some good years now. I know when we last saw her, she looked exhausted. Uncle Andy couldn't walk much on his own anymore."

"She made sure he ate, she shaved him, she cut his hair. My sister is gold. They all are," John said.

"Babe, remember when I told her maybe she should put him in a nursing home? "Tessie wouldn't hear of it. She said, I married him for better or worse."

John stood up. "I'd better call Eddie." When John got off the phone, he confirmed that Eddie would take care of all the details and get back to him.

Paula volunteered to drive, saying, "Dad, I'll drive us there. I want to pay my respects, too."

"That'll be nice, honey. You can't wait for people to die to see your relatives," he said.

"I love your subtlety, Daddy," Paula said as she went over to her father to give him a little kiss on the cheek. He was feeling low about his sister's loss, about a lot of changes beyond his control. She knew that. Besides, he was right. It would be nice to see her other cousins. Unfortunately, it seemed like the only time the entire family gathered was at funerals or weddings these days.

A funny thing about many families in those days was how they acted as though New Jersey, Brooklyn, or Staten Island were a thousand miles apart. Simple get-togethers become more like excursions, with people packing coolers, remembering to take photo albums, and behaving as though 50 miles were 200. Paula drove to Brooklyn with her father in the front seat, while her mom settled in the back with a warm blanket around her legs.

Crossing over the Verrazano Bridge, taking the Bay Ridge exit ramp to 18th Avenue, Paula looked for the funeral home. There was the awning that read Marasco Funeral Home. Paula dropped her parents off at the front door. John helped his wife out of the rear seat of the car, and Paula went to park the big Buick in the funeral parking lot. Immediately upon entering the front room, she was struck by how depressing funeral homes were. Everything about the décor, even the temperature, conspires to shout, "Unhappiness Happens Here!" The rooms are cold and the windows sealed shut with layers of curtains to block out the daylight. God forbid any sunlight should come in. "That would make the corpse look ashen," Eddie once told Paula, to which she responded, "Oh, excuuuse me—I forgot they were supposed to look healthy." He ignored her jibe and said, "We prefer the artificial pink lighting so the deceased has a healthy glow."

Adding their own cloying accent, the scent of flowers could be overwhelming, which was typical in these places. "Why do people spend so much money on flowers when a person dies, when they'd never do that for them when they're alive?" her mother rhetorically asked Paula when she caught up with them. Baskets, sprays, vases, wreaths— everywhere you looked there were flowers from relatives and friends.

"Someday," Paula thought, "I'll decorate a funeral home, and it'll look different." She mused, "Too bad I couldn't add a liquor bar for my Irish friends, and an espresso bar for my Italian friends. A jar of biscotti would be nice touch or even some miniature cannoli."

As she approached the anteroom, she could see many familiar faces: her Uncle Ernie, Aunt Catherine, Aunt Anna, even Uncle Joe, the youngest and the black sheep of the family. He seemed to be always angry at one sibling or another. At one time he had stopped speaking to her father because his mother, Angelina, sold the house to John and not to him. Paula wondered which one of the relatives would make his list this year.

The Maida family all had the same face—dark almond-shaped eyes, olive complexion, thick curly hair, and those deep-set folds between nose and mouth. Would she have them someday, she wondered? As soon as her aunts saw her, they came running over, making a big fuss. Arms flung around her. Kisses and more kisses. "Paula! Look who's here, Paula!"

"God, I love these women. How could you not?" Her Aunt Catherine stood back, holding her at arm's length, tsk-tsking, "How thin you are. Don't you eat? My God, look at her, Anna, look how thin Paula is!" She smiled her irresistible smile, wagging her finger at her niece, "You come to my house in Long Island, and I'll fix you a nice meal. I'd love to have you over." Paula knew she meant it. Her aunt had been a widow for many years. And her only daughter Carol had died a decade earlier. No one knew much about anorexia then, but she had watched Carol fret over eating even a celery stick. Imagine how well an Italian mother could tolerate such an awful disease.

From the corner of Paula's eyes, she saw her parents speaking to Aunt Tessie. Paula's aunts would have talked to her for hours, so she excused herself to pay her respects to her Aunt Tess, who was seated up front by the casket. Wearing the traditional black dress, white handkerchief in hand, her eyes were as red as her hair once was. "Aunt Tessie, I'm so sorry for your loss." She bent down and kissed her gently on the cheek.

"Paula! Oh, Paula! Look how pretty you look. I don't see you any more, how come?"

Feeling guilty, she made up some feeble excuses. "Oh, Aunt Tessie, I don't know where the time goes. And I'm managing the property where I live, plus I have to keep my eye on JB. You know he's sixteen now."

"How's JB?" she asked. "How old is he now?" Then she remembered Aunt Tessie was hard of hearing and refused to wear a hearing aid.

Her daughter, Andrea, repeated very close to her mother's ear, "JB is fine, mom. He sends his love. He's sixteen now."

Paula asked, "Andrea, when did you fly in?"

"Just yesterday," she answered. "I tell you, Paula—it's only five hours flying time, but being here is like visiting another planet."

"You're the cousin who got away," Paula said, remembering the great fondness they always enjoyed as children.

"Well, I did it the only way I could. I married a nice Italian boy who just happened to live in California," she smiled.

"Oh, Andrea, I'm so sorry we have to see each other here of all places. But I've missed you," she said impulsively. And it was true. She was only a few years younger than her cousin, but they were once close. "Andrea, how many years has it been since you left Brooklyn?"

"God, Paula, it's over twenty. I left New York University and next thing, I'm working as a secretary at an ad agency supporting a husband. Talk about a change of scenery in Los Angeles versus Brooklyn."

"Well, you don't look the worse for wear."

"Oh please," she said. "I haven't stopped crying all week. I look like shit." But to Paula, she looked like wonderful Andrea. She had her father's handsome looks—slim, long legs, and the prettiest hands she ever saw. She'd married Frank Giambrone, who seemed to be a fine young man, and terribly handsome, too. The first time Paula met him she thought he looked like the actor Troy Donahue. After a few years of marriage they split up, thankfully with no kids to share. Andrea frequently stated, "He took the china, and I took the typewriter." Paula wasn't quite sure if subtly that meant he was gay, and she was reluctant to ask her cousin that question.

"So, are you still setting the ad world on fire?" she asked.

Aunt Tessie would always tell the family how well Andrea was doing. "Andrea got named vice president." Then she paused, asking, "What is that?" "Andrea's company gave her a car. A Cadillac," and she showed everyone pictures to prove it. "Andrea just bought a house in Beverly Hills."

It was all the more remarkable to all, given the tiny three-room apartment in which Andrea and her sister were raised. The family was proud of her. The two cousins walked toward a quieter area to continue catching up. "Tell me, Paula, what's going on in your life?"

"Oh, cuz, I'm in love."

"Oh, sweetheart, how thrilling—I vaguely remember being in love once, or was that lust?" Paula was about to laugh but remembered that she was in a funeral home.

"Andrea, look, please don't let on, but I want you to meet Richard." With that, she pulled out a few photos of him with her. She loved the way they looked together, and Andrea acknowledged that very thing.

"What a gorgeous couple. Look how attractive he is! Tall and elegant. What does Mr. Wonderful do?"

She gave her the shorthand version, doing the very thing Richard had done the day they met. "He's CEO of Adidas," she said, without going into the pending "ex" of it. It might have been years since the two of them had seen each other, but that day Andrea and Paula reconnected and vowed to stay in touch. It proved to be a promise they would keep.

Chapter 20

UNEXPECTED
EVENTS

T HE LONG WINTER DAYS WERE UPON THEM, and with
the afternoons being especially dreary, Paula decided to
stop over at her folks' home to have a cup of hot tea. She
had an hour to kill before picking up JB at the high school.
She flung open the front door, and the aroma of something
sweet baking in the oven whiffed in the air—great timing.
"Hi, guys, what smells so good in here?"

"Mom just baked a cinnamon coffee cake," her father
replied. They all sat down for tea and conversation while
waiting for the cake to cool off, discussing family gossip
and food, when Marian pranced in the front door looking
extremely happy and jubilant. This in itself was a rarity, since
she harbored feelings of low self-esteem and always looked
sad.

"Hi, Sis," Paula said. "Want a cup of tea?"

"Sure," she responded. She didn't wait to sit down. "I
have some news to tell you."

Rose instinctively asked, "What's wrong?"

"No, Mom, I have good news. I'm pregnant!" Those two words filled the room with joy, laughs, tears, and hugs all around.

John threw his hands in the air as if in a chorus of Hallelujah. "Thank you, Lord! After seventeen years, finally another grandchild in this family."

Paula, rotating her hips and waving her hands, asked "When, Marian, when?"

"Dr. Bloom said sometime in early November. I just came from his office."

"Oh, you must let me decorate the baby's room. Please. It'll be so perfect. I hope it's a girl." The teapot started to whistle, as though to punctuate their euphoria!

The entire family happily planned the arrival of Marian's baby. John had something to look forward to. Paula was thinking shades of pink and looking at baby furniture. Rose was making sure Marian had all the necessities a baby needs. In the midst of all this, Paula was totally taken by surprise when one day Richard asked, "Honey Bear, what do you think if I purchase a house for us to live in? JB can have his own room and we can have room for the girls when they come to visit. Don't you think that's a good idea?"

Is he testing me?, she wondered. Nonetheless, she replied, "No, Richard, I don't think so."

"Why not?" He inquired, looking hurt.

"Well, for one thing, I'm not looking for a roommate. I'm still young, and I hope to marry again. Besides, what would my parents think?"

He seemed a little agitated, "Well, are you worried about your parents, or us?"

"Actually, I'm thinking about me. Living together isn't what I envision for myself."

Marriage was a very sensitive subject for Richard. Having two failed relationships, he swore that he would never marry again. And then Paula came along and drove him crazy—he was totally taken with her. He was in a serious dilemma. He even told his eldest son, Rich Jr., "If ever I think of marrying again, just shoot me." Months went by without any other words of marriage. But they were a partnership in other ways. They discussed purchasing real estate as investment properties, and since Paula still had her real estate license, it made perfect sense. He would finance the deals; she would decorate and then flip the property for a profit. They ventured into the city looking at apartments and both favored two at Seven Gramercy Park, which came with a key to a private park. They didn't act quickly enough, and by the time they submitted bids, the proprieties were under contracts.

Though they maintained separate residences, they spent as much time as they could together. When Richard's parents paid a visit from California, Paula made sure to invite them over to meet her family. "It's about time, Paula," Richard kidded. "I've been amply scrutinized and analyzed by your folks. Now it's the Maddens' turn."

"I'm nervous enough as it is, Richard. What will I serve? Suppose they don't like me? What do you think?"

"Are you kidding? A wonderful woman who can cook and loves their son and can afford her own townhouse just might be their dream come true," he said, laughing.

It was only natural that she wanted to impress his parents. What Paula could never have anticipated is how well Rose and John Maida and Anne and John Madden would get along. She had met Richard's parents only once before and liked his mother immediately. His father seemed stern and was a cold fish. But this fish took to her parents like water. As it turned out, they'd all come from Brooklyn.

Richard's mother had been born and grew up on the same street as Paula's mother, Sterling Place in Park Slope. The moment they made that connection, the conversation became very animated. The evening was a huge success, in Paula's estimation. It seemed like they were barely saying hello before it was time to say goodnight. Big hugs, hearty handshakes, and lots of smiles made it clear that everyone had an enjoyable time.

"Whew! One less thing out of the way," Paula exclaimed.

On a cool, brisk autumn day in October, Paula and Richard had plans to go into the city for dinner. "Let's drive in earlier," Richard suggested. "We can walk around." Since it was the eve of Yom Kippur, the traffic was light. They parked the car and proceeded to walk along Fifth Avenue, stopping in Saks Fifth Avenue, where they would both check out the latest styles in fashion. Richard never felt comfortable in stores with high prices, but Paula knew she could always locate him looking at clothes on the sale racks. Afterwards, they would cross the street and stop at St. Patrick's Cathedral to say a little prayer. That day, as Richard opened the heavy, bronze doors, he took her arm and gently escorted her down the center aisle. They sat in the front pew, and as Paula was about to kneel down and say a prayer, he took her hand into his. Looking deeply into her eyes he said very softly, "Paula, will you be my wife for the rest of my life?"

Stunned, surprised, she gazed at him for what felt like a long time, trying to absorb what he had just said. She felt tears well up in her eyes, and gently squeezed his hand, "Richard, I would love to be your last wife." She had never seen him smile more broadly.

"I love you, Honey Bear." Paula was numb, elated.

"Thank you, God," she whispered under her breath and remembered to leave an extra generous donation in the tithing box on their way out.

One of the things Paula loved about Richard was his unerring sense of occasion. "Come with me, my bride-to-be," he said like an Irish leprechaun. They celebrated with a bottle of champagne and a $21 hamburger at the Twenty-One Club.

"Oh, Richard, I can't wait to tell my parents," she gushed.

He said, "It won't come as a surprise to them, since I asked your father for your hand in marriage."

"You mean, he knew about your intentions for this evening?" She should have realized he would do something like that; her guy was a class-act. She loved him even more that evening for asking her Johnny for her hand.

The next few weeks were a happy blur. They had to announce to all of their families that they were getting married and select a date. She told JB first.

"Where are we gonna live?" he asked, apparently concerned.

"Well, we haven't decided yet; but it'll just be us three. The girls will be with us from time to time, of course."

He looked relieved. No big changes there. "Sounds good, I like Richard."

"Dad, were you surprised when Richard asked you for my hand in marriage?" she asked her father.

"He'd have to be an idiot not to, Paula, and we've seen how happy you are together."

"We knew you'd never do anything stupid like live with someone you weren't married to." Her mother weighed in.

"Well, you're right, Mom." She was taken aback by how much they had intuited.

"We have our doubts, you know that, honey," her father continued.

"But why, Dad? You like Richard! I know you do."

"It isn't that, Paula," her mother interrupted. "He's been married twice before, four kids. We can't help but wonder what went wrong."

"I . . . I don't know what to say," she stammered, feeling her balloon deflating.

"Paula, we're happy for you. Not so much because of Richard but because we know you love him and he's been good to you," her mother said, surprising Paula with her conciliatory tone.

"Your mother is right, Honey," dad said. "As long as he makes you happy, we're happy."

A month later they were wed. Paula chose the same day her parents got married forty-four years earlier.

"Whaddya say, Richard? November twenty-second?"

"Well, it's certainly worked for them," he agreed. "On the other hand, it's the date JFK was shot, you know."

"I'll take romance over politics any day, smarty pants," she said in her coolest tone.

"What happened to Huggy Bear?" he teased. Sticking to that date meant they had just one month to plan the ceremony and reception. There were some obstacles to overcome. Marian was expecting her baby in early November—would she be able to be her sister's matron of honor? Richard's ex-wife was participating in an Explorer's Club expedition, and asked him to watch the girls—that eliminated any plans they might have had for a honeymoon. But fate was on their side: the hotel room they wanted was available for that afternoon, and Marian delivered a pretty baby girl two weeks before the wedding. Laura Anne weighed in at five pounds, thirteen ounces, with fair skin and light brown hair. And in lieu of a honeymoon, they all enjoyed Thanksgiving together as a family in the small townhouse where Paula lived.

Marian looked radiant in a Chanel-style wool ivory suit, and no one would discern that she had just had a baby two weeks earlier. Richard's eldest son acted as best man. Rose's brother, Judge Carmine Marasco, presided over the ceremony, which was held in front of a majestic fire place in the Library Room of the old Villard Mansion at the Helmsley Palace Hotel in New York City. All of the children, both sets of parents, family, and friends gathered around the bride and groom—small but intimate—forty guests in all.

It was exactly what Paula had pictured. The room was elegant and richly decorated with wood-paneled walls, old woven tapestries, a curved, vaulted plaster ceiling, and thousands of old books lining the library shelves. The massive stone fireplace was decorated with fresh garlands of greens, with white and cream flowers and old English ivy cascading down the sides. When the pianist began to play Pachelbel's Canon in D, John knew it was his cue to take his daughter's arm. "Are you ready, Honey, to get married?"

She looked into his deep-set brown eyes that were her eyes, too. "More than you know, Daddy . . . I love you so much, and I love the man in that next room, too." With a tender glance, he kissed her on the cheek and proceeded to escort his daughter into the next room to give her hand to a very nervous groom.

Paula couldn't have been more pleased with the events of that day. Having labored so long as to what to wear, she was happy with her final selection. In the end she chose a simple, fitted, two-piece cream lace skirt with a scallop hem and fitted lace top with long sleeves with a sweetheart neckline. In lieu of a bridal veil, she selected a small, beaded satin cream-colored pillbox hat, with her thick, brown hair peaking out on the sides. She carried a long spray of calla lilies in her arms, wrapped in satin ribbons. The resplendent décor of the room befit the love she felt from their families and friends. Richard was everything she could have hoped for, and Paula felt gratitude that she was able to find love once again in her life. But most of all, she was elated to have the title of being a Mrs. once again, and the security that came with it.

Chapter 21

HORSES AND HEARTBREAK

Andrea called from california to extend her good wishes to her cousin. "I know you're crazy about him, Paula." As they talked, Andrea exposed her feelings on her how it made her think of her own wedding night, which was not at all what she'd expected. "We'd had such a wonderful wedding, as you know," she started.

"I remember it was an afternoon wedding," Paula interrupted.

Her cousin replied, "I was crazy about Frank, and I was so happy knowing we were husband and wife."

"He was a terrific fellow, Andrea."

"He was great. And those gorgeous green eyes. But on our wedding night after we'd made love, I remember lying in bed listening to him snore a little and staring up at the ceiling. 'What have I done,' is all I could think. I felt trapped. I would be married for the rest of my life, and here I was only twenty. Do you think other newlyweds feel that way?"

Paula didn't know. That wasn't how she remembered her wedding night with Tom or with Richard. "I had a blissful wedding night at the Helmsley Palace," she told Andrea. But she left out that there was the one moment during which she caught her new husband gazing out the window looking at the sun coming up, so pensive. "He must be anxious, this is his third marriage." That's probably it, she imagined.

One of the first things the newlyweds realized was that they needed a larger space to all live together. Paula once again relished the thought of decorating another home, this time for both of them and their newly combined families. When she told Richard what she had in mind, he was all for it.

"That would be great, Paula . . . we need a fresh start together."

"Fresh is what you get with me," she said, as she gave him a big kiss.

"I love fresh women," he said, hoping to take this action further. But his new wife was eager to tell him about the interesting property that captured her imagination. It was a rustic style log house complete with a barn, an open fenced infield for horses situated on seven acres of heavily wooded land in Warren, New Jersey, about twenty-five minutes west from her townhouse. This piece of real estate conjured up visions of a bucolic gentry's life. Her wheels started to spin. "Richard, I could make this house into something really special for us." With solid Brooklyn–Jersey roots, the decision to go really rural was a new adventure for Paula. She loved the expanse of the property, and she thought Richard was such a manly guy that it seemed right for him to live where corduroy jackets with suede at the elbows fit right in. He even enjoyed an occasional pipe with cherry blend tobacco with an aroma that enhanced his masculinity, in her mind.

"It needs work, Paula, don't you think?" he asked tentatively when they viewed it.

"Of course it does, but if we can buy it at the right price, think of the value of the land." They made an offer, and it was accepted. Within weeks, the renovations began—a new kitchen, restyling the massive, brick fireplace in the living room, the addition of a master suite. They worked as a team with Richard's money and her vision.

Paula had mixed emotions about moving out of her comfortable home. It had provided her personal solace after Tom's passing. "What'll become of it now?" she wondered. "Dad, I hate to sell this place. It's been such a comfortable home for JB and me." She thought about her options and wasn't pleased with any of them. She really didn't want to sell and couldn't just rent it to strangers. Being very selective and fastidious, the thought of strangers in her home wasn't acceptable. "They'd never take care of it the way I do." For a brief few minutes her father was silent.

"Honey, how would you like to have mom and me for tenants?"

"Are you serious, Daddy?

"You know, kiddo, Mom and I aren't getting any younger. Houses are work—lawn care, shoveling snow, and I also have your mom to care for. Living in a condo will be easier for us." Paula knew this was a terrific idea as soon as he said it.

"Oh Dad, no wonder you're my hero. You always come up with perfect solutions, always. That would be fabulous!" Leave it to her father to make everything work for everyone. It really made perfect sense for all of them. Her mother loved the idea of living in a small community. It was close to grocery stores and the hospital, and in the summer Rose could sit in the backyard that Paula had landscaped. It was reminiscent of a miniature Tuscan style garden, with vines, roses, and a brick patio laid in a herringbone design.

John suggested, they would pay their daughter a rent, as well as pay all of the utilities. At first Paula refused, but John insisted. "Save the money for JB's schooling," he told her. Within two months after listing their home on Elm Street, they had a buyer. John felt like he hit the jackpot when their listing real estate agent, a friend of Paula's, informed them that a couple made a solid offer with no contingencies. And which netted them a hefty profit. Several months later, they all moved into their respective new residences. Rose and John relocated into the comfortable townhouse, while Paula, Richard, and JB moved west to the "Bear Ranch."

"Mom, you gotta be kidding. He's Huggy Bear. You're Honey Bear. And now this is Bear Ranch? What the heck am I, Baby Bear?"

"I like living in a house with a name, Twin Oaks, Bear Ranch," Paula replied.

"Nut Farm," he teased.

Richard was pleased with what his wife had accomplished in such a short period of time. It turned out exactly how Paula had envisioned. The living room had large, picture windows that overlooked the fields. Comfortable furnishings were covered in warm, brick-colored corduroy fabric and Tartan plaids on the swivel chairs that flanked the fireplace, with each chair sporting a needlepoint pillow of dogs, and linen floral curtains with five-inch flax bullion fringe. Rose gave her daughter lots of family sterling silver in her move, and it shined in the rooms when the sun peered through.

"Paula, this is so me," Richard said when she showed him his completed office. She decorated it with the things he loved: an old rolltop desk, a worn leather chair, lots of photographs of his children, his collection of books and nineteenth century prints of famous Irish race horses hanging on the glazed green walls. The room definitely had the handsome feel of a man's study.

Shortly after they moved into the ranch, two young ladies came to their front door to ask them if they could rent out the stables for their horses. This was a decorating idea that Paula hadn't even thought of when they purchased the property. The girls owned three horses and would tend to their needs three times a day. Would they be interested? Paula was thrilled with the idea. With three new tenants—Bird, Appy, and Sissy Bell—Paula felt like she had stepped into an *Architectural Digest Country Living* issue. When she told Richard about the horses, he laughed. "Paula, they're horses, not furniture."

"But aren't they perfect?" she enthused.

"OK, but they better clean up after them." She didn't particularly like the tone of his voice, and lately she noticed he was becoming moody.

One day, out of the blue, he snapped at her, "Please don't bother me when I'm in my office. It's my workday. I need privacy."

"Okay, Huggy Bear, I won't bother you."

Then Richard started making belittling comments to her such as, "Paula you're turning into a maid around here," when he would see her cleaning the house.

"You know I like a clean home, Richard. With so much dirt outside we track it into the house on our shoes." They hadn't landscaped the property yet. But she chalked his callousness up to the fact that he seemed increasingly stymied on where his life was going. Since he couldn't play golf in the winter months, life on the ranch wasn't exactly exciting for him. Soon he started excluding Paula, becoming preoccupied with his daughters.

"I want to spend more quality time with them," he announced.

"Okay, Richard, I understand," she said hesitantly, not at all sure that she did.

"Glad you do. I'm taking Mara skiing."

"Would you like me to go with you?" she asked.

"No, you don't ski anyway," he curtly replied. They had only been married two months, and he didn't even tell her where they'd be staying. "I'll call you when we get there." He called four days later.

To make matters worse, even JB was picking up on Richard's sudden change. "Hey, Mom, what's going on with you and Rich these days?

"What are you talking about?"

"He's acting weird lately, and yesterday he yelled at me and said I was on the phone too much."

"Oh, Honey, be patient with him. This is an adjustment for all of us. We can't be a family overnight. It's going to take time." She was trying hard to reassure her son, as well as herself. But deep down inside, she felt something indeed was wrong. But what? If her son could sense it, she knew her parents could, too.

"Paula, for a newlywed, you're spending a lot of time at our house these days," her mother quipped.

"Gee, Mom, do you think Dad is the only family member who's crazy about Laura?" she replied, trying to make light of it. Marian routinely took the baby over every afternoon to be with her grandparents. Baby Laura was cherished and coddled by her grandfather. John called her "Chicken Dinner," because she was smaller than a small roasting chicken when she came home from the hospital. She mesmerized him; John had another little Paula to dote on.

Eventually, Paula hated to admit to her family that things were not what she had anticipated her married life to be with Richard. "Daddy, Richard is having a difficult time adjusting to married life."

"Hell, sweetheart, he's been married enough; he should be a champion at it by now." Her father's mouth was tightly set; she knew he hated to hear that anything was amiss.

Her mom was quick to add, "Paula, I told you Richard wasn't ready for marriage. It was too soon, you were so anxious."

"Mom, what are you saying, that I forced him into marrying me?"

"No, dear, that's not what I mean, but he's a complex person and you didn't see all the red flags."

She left there feeling miserable. It wasn't any better when she returned to the ranch. "Dinner's ready, Richard."

"Great, I'm starving."

"JB, dinner's ready."

"In a minute, Mom." Afterwards, her son would take off with his friends or go upstairs and do his homework, while Richard watched sports on television. If no sports were on, he'd read or listen to music in the living room, drinking wine until it was time to go to bed. Paula was definitely confused with her husband's behavior. She tried to talk to him about his feelings, but he'd have no part of it. Also, she wasn't thrilled with their hot-cold, sexual but not communicative relationship.

Not knowing what to do, Paula suggested that Richard visit his oldest son, who had just moved to Oregon. Hoping that the trip would get him out of his funk, she needed time to be alone and get a handle on what was going on. What she was really hoping was that he would say, "Great Paula, why don't you come along?" But he didn't.

Paula was baffled with the way Richard was treating her, and the stress of their daily life together was beginning to play havoc with her mind. She felt like she was living with a different man, feeling insecure, lonely, and unloved. She wanted the man she had fallen in love with back. Where had he gone? She knew he had lots of girlfriends in his past. Was he thinking about one of them or his ex-wife? Was he sorry he married her? There were so many questions and no concrete answers. When Richard returned from Oregon, she worked up the courage to ask, "Richard, do you still love me?"

"I think I do."

"What kind of an answer is that?" she said sharply. "You think you do? Either you love me or you don't!"

"Aw, hell, Paula. I don't know what to say. I'm not happy. Half the time I have knots in my stomach, wondering what's gonna set you off, make you nervous. Everything has to be perfect with you: the perfect meal, the perfect house, even the perfect lay!"

She was reeling. She couldn't comprehend what the hell he was babbling about—he was finding fault with everything: that she didn't ski, didn't like the opera, didn't like his friends, and they didn't have much in common. Finally, to appease his wife, he agreed to go with her to a marriage counselor.

In their joint sessions, Richard would say things like, "Paula is good for me today, but will she be good for me ten years from now?" or, "Doctor, we have nothing in common." In a private session, Dr. Saffron told Paula that her husband was having a mid-life crisis. "And the fact that he enjoys alcohol doesn't help his mood swings," the doctor added. And now to top things off, Richard also started talking about his concerns over financial matters, which Paula figured was probably provoked by his ex-wife's suspicion that he held out on her when he sold his business.

"My ex-wife is suing me for a ton of money. She feels she's entitled to more money from the sale of the business," Richard had told Paula.

"Dad, I love Richard, and I don't want to lose him. I told him early on that divorce was not in my vocabulary. I don't know what's happened to him," Paula cried to her father.

"Honey, you've been through worse things than this in your life. Hang in there. You know Mom and I will always be here for you."

She kissed his forehead and squeezed his hand, "I know you will, Dad, I love you sooo much."

Day after day, week after week, it was the same. Finally, Paula decided to stop going for counseling. "Dr. Saffron, I won't be coming to you anymore, with or without Richard." To her surprise, the doctor agreed with her.

"Paula, think of yourself first. Richard has put you on the backburner for now. Confront him with reality," she advised.

"Huh? What does that mean?" Paula asked her bluntly.

"Don't let him boss you around. Be your own person."

Paula left there in a fog. What was she telling me? Was she on my side or his? Am I getting paranoid too? Now she was really perplexed. After many restless months of trying to sort things through, Paula decided Dr. Saffron was right. It's my life, too! What do I want to do? Certain that it wasn't catering to Richard anymore, she was physically and emotionally tired of trying to make things work out. It takes two people to have a relationship; that she was sure of. Even though she had so much emotionally invested in this marriage, she was determined it would not ruin her life.

As her mother was fond of saying, "It's not how you start up in life that matters, it's how you end up that counts."

Chapter 22

♥

IT'S A SHORT WALK
IN THE PARK

"LIFE IS SURE DIFFICULT, DAD, ISN'T IT?" Paula moaned one evening to her father. John's life was certainly not what he had bargained for. The previous month, Rose had fallen down and fractured her wrist, then after that she'd had a gallbladder attack and needed surgery.

Having just put his wife to bed, John was pouring them a glass of wine.

"Honey, it's the only life you get. The glass can be half full or half empty," he repeatedly said. With that, raising his glass up to hers, he said, *"A salud."*

"What else do you know, Dad?"

"What do you mean, honey?"

"I mean, here you are in your late sixties. What do you think you've learned in your life?"

"That's a great question, Paula." He paused for a moment before saying, "One thing I know is that all the rules are not fair. Good people die young. Crooks don't get caught. It never turns out the way you thought when you were young."

Paula responded, "Then how can you talk about half full, Dad?"

"It's how you look at things, sweetheart. I live in a nice home. Your mother and I have had a good marriage, two wonderful daughters. I have JB and Laura. I don't want for anything."

"But you're stuck here caring for mom day after day," Paula spoke softly. "I know you'd love to travel."

"Honey, I make the best of it. You have to or you'll drive yourself crazy." His face was so sweet, his words so loving; Paula adored this man.

"Dad, you're a dinosaur. They don't make men like you anymore." With that, she grabbed her coat, saying, "I better go now, Richard and JB are probably wondering what happened to me."

"Then drive carefully, honey, and remember, it's a short walk in the park."

"What is, Dad?"

"Life, sweetheart, life."

Paula's short walk in the park took a detour one day soon after that. While drying herself off from a long, hot shower, she felt a lump the size of an egg, under her armpit.

She panicked and headed straight for her parents' home. Her father had gone out grocery shopping, for which she was grateful. She needed to see her mother.

"Mom, what is this?" Her voice noticeably very frightened, she lifted her up arm to show her the lump. Rose touched it very gingerly. Her face became tense.

"Whatever it is, it doesn't belong there. I'll give you the name of a doctor. Call him now."

Richard was kind and caring and offered to take his wife to the doctor's office. "Thanks, Huggy, but that's the day you promised Mara you'd drive her to school."

"Damn," he uttered. His oldest daughter was starting a private boarding school, Northfield–Mount Herman, in the hills of Massachusetts. Mara desperately wanted to go there, insisting her current school wasn't challenging enough, plus she didn't enjoy living at home with her mother. After giving it a great deal of consideration and calculating the financial consequences, Richard agreed. "She's got a wonderful mind, Paula," he said earnestly. "I'd love to give her every opportunity to shine; anyway, I think the distance away from her mother will be good for her."

Paula really didn't mind his driving his daughter that day, and told him so. "It's okay, really, I'll be perfectly fine. Dad will drive me." A week later Paula was scheduled for surgery to remove an enlarged lymph node under her arm. Since John insisted his daughter needed TLC, and lots of her mother's good home cooking, Richard brought Paula to their home immediately after the surgery to recuperate.

A few days later the surgeon called to report on the pathology report, "Paula, I initially suspected you might have Hodgkin's lymphoma, but I'm glad to say that the report came back with no malignancy; instead, features consistent of toxoplasmosis were present." Hearing the good news, the family was immediately relieved. John made a special visit to church to give thanks for the positive outcome. Later Paula found out that toxoplasmosis was a single-cell parasite infected cats carry. How did she get this, she wondered? They didn't have a cat.

"Richard, do you think I could have picked this up here at the ranch?"

"Whaddya talking about?" he responded brusquely.

"Well, you know the previous owners had lots of animals, including several cats." "Beats me," he said.

But Paula remembered doing lots of gardening work that summer, including planting dozens of geranium flowers all along the side of the driveway, only to wake up the next morning to find that the deer had nibbled the tops off every flower she planted. They had lots of little creatures where they lived, including a scorpion look-a-like she found in the bathroom once. This little health scare re-enforced what she had been thinking.

Paula had to face the obvious; life in the country was not what she had anticipated.

BIG MISTAKE! Neither one of them was enjoying this home. It felt utterly false and pretentious. She firmly believed she had to follow her gut feeling; an inner voice was talking to her. "Richard, I'm sorry, but I don't enjoy living here, and I want to move. It's not what I expected, and quite honestly I don't think you're happy here, either."

"What are you suggesting?" he asked, curious to find out what she had in mind.

"I'm saying that I want to sell this property and move on, perhaps go to school and pursue a career in interior design."

"Where do you want to go?" he inquired.

"I'm not sure, but I was thinking of renting an apartment in Manhattan, at least for a while. And you, Richard, where will you go?" Her question threw him for a loop.

After a lengthy silence, he looked up at her with great tenderness in his eyes. "I'll live anywhere with you, Paula. I know I have been acting like a jerk, but I really do love you, honey bear."

Hearing these words, Paula felt a weight of emotions lifted from her chest. She had been so afraid that Richard was drifting away from her. Their marriage was all that mattered. His comment reassured her that their relationship had promise. He still loved her, yet he had no idea how much damage he had done to her heart. She was still mystified by his callous treatment of her.

Later that evening Richard asked Paula, "And what about JB and the girls?" He apparently was still thinking about their earlier conversation to move into New York City.

"JB is talking about getting a job, and maybe rooming with a friend. I think it's only a matter of time before he moves out. We can rent an apartment with an extra bedroom for either of them."

"That sounds good, something different for us. Alone time," he grinned mischievously. Honestly, Paula couldn't figure her husband out at times.

Chapter 23

FEELING BLUE—
THROW A PARTY

S ELLING A UNIQUE PROPERTY like the Bear Ranch
would take time. Paula realized that a small horse ranch
has a limited market, but the time could be used to her
advantage. They needed to gather information as to where
they would like to live, decide what design school she would
attend, and give her parents ample time to adjust to this news.
In the meantime, her father was approaching his seventieth
birthday. More than anything, he needed to have a pick-me-
up. From his stooping shoulders to his slowing gait, everything about him looked dejected. His last birthday had come
and gone without much fanfare, and this year Paula wanted
it to be different. Wanting to acknowledge how important
and significant his life was to his family, she thought a party
would certainly lift his spirits.

"Richard," she announced after mulling it over, "I want
to throw a party for Dad."

"What kind of a party did you have a mind?"

She didn't waste a minute telling him exactly what was on her mind. "I want to celebrate it in a big way, in a local restaurant with his family."

Richard surprised her once again with his generosity. "Paula, if you want to throw a party for your dad, I'll pay for it. Let's talk about who you'd invite."

"The whole family, Aunt Catherine, Aunt Tessie, Aunt Anna, Uncle Ernie, cousins, Mom's brothers, and their old friends from Brooklyn." She ran the idea by Marian, who immediately thought it was an excellent suggestion.

But Marian had one misgiving. "Paula, I'm not sure Mom is up to going to a party and staying up late. What do you think?

"I think if we give her extra pain medication and make sure she sits most of the evening, she'll do fine."

Marian added enthusiastically, "We better remember to bring her pillow for her to sit on. Who knows, an evening like this may be good for her."

"Well, it sure as hell will be good for Dad," Paula replied.

They now had a game plan; even JB was getting into the act. He asked to make sure that the restaurant had a piano so he could entertain at the party. He agreed that they would need a DJ as well because the little Italian aunts all loved to dance.

"Let's make sure the DJ has Dean Martin's version of "Volare" and Mom's favorite, "Danke Schoen" sung by Wayne Newton," Marian interjected.

A restaurant in a neighboring town was getting good reviews for its food; it had a nicely decorated back room for private parties that could easily accommodate about fifty people. Paula met with the owner and selected the menu, arranged for fresh flowers on the tables, and planned for lots of votive candles for the round tables of eight. Two weeks before the party, she insisted that her parents go with Richard and her to get their passports. She told them there was no specific reason except that it gave them the freedom to pick up and go somewhere.

"Paula," her father said forlornly, "Where we gonna go? The doctor's office?"

"Humor me, Dad," she said.

"I have from the day you were born," he answered, smiling at his own joke. Fortunately, her mother was feeling up to it on the appointed day and was a good sport about it. "I agree with your father," she said from the backseat of the car. "The only trip we'll be taking is to this passport office and home again."

"Mom, you never had a passport. How old are you? Pretend you're taking a trip. Who knows? It could happen." Richard and Paula talked about taking her parents to Italy as a birthday present for John. She compiled a photo album to present to him the evening of the party along with a travel brochure entitled "A Roman Holiday," complete with Alitalia baggage tags. The remaining empty pages were marked, "Photos to Come—La Famiglia In Italy."

The big night came amid a flurry of whispered phone calls and invitations sent out to everyone. Paula told her parents that the immediate family wanted to take them to a new restaurant for dinner. Rose insisted she'd rather stay home and have a quiet dinner with the family. But the tightly knit group held firm.

"C'mon, Mom, let's go out for Daddy's birthday. Don't be a party pooper. Put on your party dress and let Marian fix your hair."

She smiled. "Are you up to something, Paula?"

That evening both Rose and John took special care to dress appropriately; they were told they were going to a first-class restaurant and that they should dress to impress. It had been some time since Rose had seen her husband wearing a suit, and for this evening John chose his dark gray pin-stripe suit, perfectly starched white shirt, and a beautiful silver tie. With his olive complexion and gray hair, the overall effect was distinguished and handsome. When she saw her husband, Rose teased, "Babe, you have a date with someone special?"

"Yep," he said gamely. "Name is Rose, a hot ticket."

Richard chimed in, "Rose, you look gorgeous."

Indeed, Rose looked lovely in a teal-colored silk dress, a touch of coral blush on her sallow cheeks, and a hint of pink lipstick. Marian made sure she gave her mom that special glow for this occasion. Only her rickety walk and her dark, orthopedic shoes were a dead giveaway to her condition. But her family chose to concentrate on the ankles-up this evening. When the family arrived at the restaurant, the maitre d' acknowledged that their table was ready and asked them to follow him. Walking past the many full tables of diners in the main part of the restaurant, Rose turned to her daughter and asked rather loudly, "Where the heck is he taking us?"

Hearing her comment, the maitre d' said, "Just a little room your daughter requested." Then he opened the double doors to the crowd of familiar faces inside.

Everyone yelled in unison, "Surprise! Happy Birthday, John!" Rose and John turned toward each other simultaneously in utter amazement.

"Babe, did you know about this?" he asked his wife. Before she could reply, people converged around them, with kisses and more kisses. Each new face registered a surprise.

"Tessie! Katy! Ernie! Oh my God, look there's Jeanette and Frank and my nephews." People they hadn't seen for a while. Tears rolled down from John's eyes, as he took out his white handkerchief to dry his cheeks. "My family! My sisters!" The only one who couldn't make it was his sister Anna. Now wheelchair-bound, her right leg had been amputated a few months ago. Her diabetes had caused complications, resulting in gangrene. In spite of her doctor's warnings for years, she refused to stop drinking or smoking. But she was still sharp as a pistol. Even in a wheelchair, she still requested her cigarettes and a Beefeater martini. Both Tessie and Catherine, on the other hand, never drank. They were first and foremost interested in food.

From the corner of Paula's eye, she watched her aunts taking several hors d'oeuvres each time a waiter came around with different trays. By the time they sat down to dinner, they attacked the bread, rolls, and everything on their plate with euphoric gusto. "Look at my sisters," John smiled broadly. "You'd think they'd never seen food. Those two . . . they've always been like that."

Rose said, "They eat like there's no tomorrow."

The party was enjoyed by all, especially the older generation, who spent hours reminiscing about lost friends, who was and who wasn't living anymore. "Whatever happened to crazy Lucy, or Eddie-boy?" Rose was holding up well. Wayne reported to Marian that he had just refreshed her drink, a Bailey's Irish Cream, and she was talking to her brother Alex and his wife.

"Won't Mommy and Daddy be surprised when they open their present from Paula: a trip to Italy?" Marian said softy to Wayne.

"I just hope your mom doesn't fall out of her chair," he answered. When John opened his present from his family, he was awestruck. "Oh, this is too much! No, I can't accept this, it's too much. Look, Angel, it's a trip to Italy for us."

His best friend, Frank, called out, "Accept it! My kids gave me a rocking chair for my birthday. What the hell do they think, we're old or something?" Everyone laughed. The DJ played, "For He's a Jolly Good Fellow."

By midnight, fifty or so very contented people bid each other a happy goodnight. Paula and Richard took her parents home and slept over. The following morning Paula awoke to sounds in the kitchen, and the aroma of a freshly brewed pot of coffee. She went downstairs to see her father in the kitchen preparing a breakfast tray to bring up to his wife, along with her pills. "Paula, what a wonderful surprise, but you and Richard shouldn't have spent so much money on a party for me."

"And why not, Dad? Didn't you have a good time?"

"Good time? I had the time of my life. The evening went by so quickly, I hated to say goodnight to everyone. And Richard gave such an eloquent toast."

"Now is the important question, Dad. Will you and Mom take the trip with us to Italy?"

"Honey, I don't want you to get upset, but mom and I discussed it this morning. There's no way she can be on a plane all those hours. She would be so stiff and uncomfortable. It just can't happen. She can barely move this morning."

"Well lemme ask you, Daddy. How about if just the three of us go? Marian can watch mommy."

"Honey, I can't leave your mom. You know how much I've been longing to go to Italy. It's always been a dream of mine. When I was a kid, my parents talked about the old country and their homes, the olive groves in the backyard, and the vineyards. I would love to make this trip, but it's not going to happen. It's just not in the cards for me." Of course, his daughter understood, but she would find a way to make this happen for her father. She would find a way!

Chapter 24

♥

THE ROAD TO
TIPPERARY

HOW DOES AN ITALIAN-AMERICAN MALE whose only dream is to visit his parents' birthplace end up in Ireland? No, a nutcase travel agent had nothing to do with it. Two weeks after the birthday party, John was still talking about what a fun time he had that evening.

"Paula, did you taste the baked clams *oreganata* or the spaghetti *carbonara*? And what was that veal dish I liked?"

"Oh, you mean *vitello rustica*, Dad? It's a sauteed veal cutlet with onions, crumbled sausage, and eggplant on top."

"Yeh, that's it. Did you see the way Wayne dug into it? I wasn't sure he was gonna come up for air."

"Hey, you were doing a pretty good job yourself. I saw you having a second helping of the sausage and peppers."

"Oh, that reminds me" John said, "Tony is coming over Thursday night for dinner." "What happened? Did the race track run out of food?" Tony was a race track aficionado, and followed the horses.

John smiled at his daughter, "No, smarty pants, he likes coming over."

"Well, of course, he does. He drinks your booze, eats your food, and when he gets too inebriated or tired, he stays over. What's not to like?"

True, John's nephew had an ingratiating personality, but he seemed to take more than he gave. That's what irked Paula most of all about her cousin; to her knowledge he never once offered to take her parents out to dinner. She detested the fact that he never put his hand in his pocket to pick up a tab, but apparently he had money to play the horses. But this was not the time for her to be petty, she thought. She knew her father needed all the diversions he could get these days.

"Mom, how ya feeling lately?" she asked.

"You don't want to know," Rose answered. "Look at my hands, I have no mobility. They hurt terribly, and I can't even hold a spoon or wear my wedding band."

"Oh Mom," Paula said, taking her hands ever so delicately into her own. Rose's once elegant hands looked more like lobster claws, with swollen knuckles and joints. Nodules protruded from her skin and took on a bluish-white tint. She could hardly move her thumbs. Marian even confided to Paula that their mother needed help in the bathroom. "Mom, what does Dr. Miller say about your hands?"

"He says I have advanced stages of rheumatoid arthritis, and he suggested I have hand surgery to correct the deformity. He said it would give me some mobility back."

"Really?" Paula hadn't heard anything about this. "Are you thinking of having it done?"

"I think so, I think so," Rose said, her mouth forming the downward turn of tears coming on.

Rose eventually had the surgery and came home with stainless steel pins in her hands. Thankfully, John hired a nurse's aide to help his wife. Nell, a short, hefty woman with a robust laugh and strong hands, came from the Dominican Republic. She was able to take care of Rose's personal needs, while John ended up cooking for the both of them. Paula's father was tired, irritable, and his wit was increasingly turning into sarcasm.

"Now I have high blood pressure," he said one day. "God isn't through pissing me off." Even Marian noticed his patience was wearing thin. "Go home now, Marian," he'd tell her. "Don't you have to cook for Wayne?" Or, "Laura is tired. Bring her home for a nap." John was displaying a bitterness that troubled his daughters.

"Richard, dad needs a vacation, a change of scenery. Something to get him out of this lousy rut he's in. Any suggestions?" Paula asked. Richard thought about it for a moment. She always loved watching him think and solve problems. She could practically see his mind coming up with various solutions and either discarding them or giving them a second thought.

"Honey Bear," he said with a look that left no doubt that he was proud of himself, "I think I have the answer. Since my mother passed away—jeez, it's already a year—I've talked about taking my father to Ireland. Hell, he'd love it. He'd get to visit his roots and, God knows, have a brew or two. How about if we take both fathers? They'd each have a built-in roommate."

"Hugs, that's brilliant!" She immediately got excited about the possibilities a trip like that would present for everyone. "Yes! We'll take the boys to Ireland."

"Right. Your dad is now seventy. Mine's, what, eighty-three? The boys?" Richard laughed.

"Richard, I love you for thinking of that," Paula said, feeling a lightness she hadn't felt in a long time, and quickly planted a kiss on his cheek.

"Hey, what kind of kiss is that for a brilliant guy like me?" he ribbed. "I'd hate to see what I got for a lousy idea."

Paula was feeling giddy at the prospect of telling her father about this plan. Then she stopped herself. "Richard, what do we do about my mom? Dad would never agree to leave her alone."

"Give me more than a peck on the cheek, and I just may come up with a plan," he teased. She did—and he did. For more than a peck, she got a perfect plan.

"Dad, when's the next time you're taking mom to her doctor?"

"Which one?" John replied.

"Her primary one for her arthritis."

"You mean Dr. Whelan, her rheumatologist? Next week some time."

"Well, you stay home. I'll take her. I have a few questions I want to ask him."

Her father seemed grateful to have one less doctor's appointment to keep.

"Good honey, that's good. It'll give me a chance to go to the barber."

The following week Paula took her mom to see Dr. Whelan. While Rose was in another room having her blood work done, Paula spoke to him privately. "Dr. Whelan, I'll be blunt. I need your help. My father has been my mother's caretaker for almost ten years, and he desperately needs a break. Can you suggest a place to park my mom for a week or so? I want to take my dad on a vacation. I was thinking of Ireland." He didn't speak for a minute, which concerned Paula. Had she been too blunt with her question?

And then he replied, "Beautiful country, Ireland is. Well, you know, Ms. Mooney . . ." "Please, call me Paula" she interrupted.

"Paula, I had an aunt with a chronic illness like your mother. It physically accelerated my uncle's decline. Let me see what I can do. I'll get back to you."

Several days later Dr. Whelan called with the results of Rose's blood work. "Paula, your mom's titers are very high, and she has tested positive for systemic lupus and Lyme disease."

"Titers? What the heck is that? Lupus? Lyme disease?" she asked, alarm building in her tone.

"Paula," he answered wryly, "I think she needs to check into the hospital for more testing. Then we can better determine what's going on."

"But she really has tested positive for all this stuff, right?" she asked suspiciously. He assured her that was absolutely the case. The hospital stay was optional, but given their recent conversation, he heartily recommended it. Apparently telling this piece of information to Rose was not so terrible. For some reason, she found comfort in going to the hospital. She had great admiration for the work that nurses performed.

"Paula, these women are amazing," she'd say with utter respect. Maybe it went back to her younger days when she wanted so desperately to become a nurse, and her family forbade her. John understood his wife's frailty and comfort zones. "Bless your mother. Going to the hospital is like staying at a Ritz Carlton. I think the Ritz would be cheaper," he added. For her part, Rose was thrilled when her family told her they wanted to take John on the trip to Ireland with Richard's father.

"Paula, the timing is perfect. Marian can take care of things at home. And your father can certainly use a vacation." Rose may have been physically ill, but her mind was fully intact.

She understood what was going on, and she had her own guilt about how much of his time and energy was tending to her needs. Now she could do something for him. Knowing that he desperately needed a break, her encouragement was all he needed.

That's how John became Sean O'Maida from County Calabria, as he introduced himself at the Laurels Pub in Killarney. The proprietor, Con O'Leary, told both fathers that they were the luckiest guys on earth to have children show them the "old sod." And to toast this occasion, he took out a bottle of vodka that was a gift from the Russian National Soccer Team, apparently from a raucous party the night before. The two men ended up as very compatible roommates throughout the trip. Paula was happy that her father was enjoying himself; every day there was something new on the agenda, thanks to Richard's traveling skills.

They stayed at Kathleen's Country Inn in Killarney, where the innkeeper looked like a young Maureen O'Hara. John would tease and praise the pretty proprietor every morning while waiting for an Irish breakfast of hot oatmeal, and then bangers and eggs with toast. In the evening, a pint or two of Guinness at Gaby's or Foley's and a good night's sleep paved the way for the next day of touring, eating, and lots of hearty laughter.

During visits to Galway and Connemara, the area of the Madden clan, the men ate dozens of oysters and drank Guinness at Moran's at the Weir in Kilcolgan. Many of the country roads had cows strolling down the streets with bells ringing on their necks. The two elderly gents followed Paula and Richard everywhere like two school boys, and always in anticipation of their next meal.

Touring the Dingle Peninsula, the four dined at Doyle's by the sea and ate freshly caught black sole. They walked the beach at Inch and watched air gliders land on the shore, consumed lots of Guinness at the Parknasilla Great Southern Hotel on the Ring of Kerry, and inhaled platters of smoked salmon on buttered toast. They kissed the Blarney Stone, flirted with the colleens at Bunratty Castle's medieval banquet, and befriended many of the patrons at Durty Nelly's and Adare Manor. They walked the Cliffs of Moher and visited numerous landmarks throughout their journey.

Dr. Whelan was right about Ireland. The countryside was pure magic to behold, with rolling green hills, sheep peacefully grazing, and stone fences as far as the eye could see. The drive along the Irish coastline was invigorating. The air was clean, and you could smell the sea. Every new town was another little adventure. With this prescription, how could Paula's Johnny not improve his mental outlook?

Chapter 25

FROM THE
COUNTRY TO
THE CITY

THE AFTERGLOW OF THE IRISH HOLIDAY was still
being touted by all that fall season, and eventually John
was back to his care-taking duties for his ailing wife. Paula
was still set on moving to New York City, eager to leave the
Bear Ranch. As she garnered from their holiday: it was one
thing to visit the bucolic countryside, but it was another to
live there day after day. Life in Warren was not stimulating
enough for either of them. Richard needed constant stimu-
lation, as she had found out the hard way. She established
that he was a high-frequency kind of guy. Perhaps that's why
his other marriages failed; his previous wives didn't get this
about him.

With the property listed, they just had to wait for the
right buyer to come along. Since the present real estate market was in the doldrums, there was no way of knowing how
long it would take to sell. Finally, six months later and after

several open houses, a man in his sixties and a buxom blonde about age forty fell in love with the property. The couple appreciated the way the house was decorated and even asked if the horses went with the sale. Paula informed them that two girls owned the horses and rented the stalls. She was sure that the girls would want the animals to stay, and would be happy to inquire for them.

Richard let Paula know that wherever she wanted to live in the city would be acceptable to him. He really didn't know much about Manhattan, and trusted her judgment. For that she was grateful. But Paula knew exactly where she would look—Sutton Place. She found a generously proportioned rental apartment with two large bedrooms and two and a half baths. Its most striking feature was its knock-out views of the East River. As her cousin Andrea said when she visited them, "So this is what being on top of the world feels like!" Best of all, it was within walking distance to the school in which Paula was enrolling, the New York School of Interior Design. Eagerly anticipating this change, both Paula and Richard looked forward to the frenetic pace of living in New York City.

The day before the moving van arrived, the couple decided to stay with Paula's parents in New Jersey. It was a warm, summer day, and with the living room windows open, Paula overheard her father talking outside to one of the neighbors.

"Susan, I'm losing my daughter."

"Whaddya mean? Is she sick?" the neighbor asked, clearly alarmed.

"No, she's moving to New York City."

When he came inside, Paula responded, "Dad, I'm not moving that far away. It's only twenty-five miles. We have two bedrooms, and you and Mom can stay over. Wait and see. You will be over plenty of times." She hadn't even left yet, and he was missing her presence already.

The last time Paula had lived in Manhattan, her life was as different as uptown from downtown. Tom had been just forty-one, and terminally ill. It was a sad end to a marriage that seemed to bring out the best in all of them, including having a son. This time around, Paula's husband was healthy and strong. In the past two years that they had been married, she had learned many things about Richard, his good traits as well as his bad. Boredom and booze proved to be his nemeses. It undermined their relationship and had to be controlled. In foresight, she couldn't help but remember her last weeks with Tom. It was such a frightening time for her, but she had found comfort living in a city with so many resources.

Residing on an island with millions of inhabitants, the city didn't seem to care about anyone's personal woes. It moved to its own pulse, its own rhythm of non-stop bustling, horns honking, and then oases of tranquility when you'd least expect them. Parks dotted the landscape, beckoning with their cascading waterfalls, iron tables, and chairs. Shops were adorned with come-hither windows of carefully merchandised fashion, blank-eyed mannequins, and a festoon of ribbon or lights. There were days when she loved losing herself in the streetscape. She particularly enjoyed taking the bus that traveled along York Avenue past Sutton Place, a splendid street parallel to the East River. It was on the bus that she would fantasize about how wonderful it would be to live in this pocket of the city. It seemed that nothing could possibly go wrong behind its door-manned buildings.

Sutton Place was an enclave for the affluent set. The society decorator Dorothy Draper once lived there. I'd like to live there someday, Paula had thought, if Tom gets well. The street was wide and had a row of brick townhouses with exquisitely carved wood doors. The townhouse on the corner had a statue of St. Francis of Assisi inside its wrought iron front gate. This small section of the street was reminiscent of a European town, especially Sutton Square at the end of 58th Street. Then there was One Sutton Place South, a majestic building designed by Rosario Candela (an Italian American architect who achieved prominence for his apartment buildings in New York City). Although it was only thirteen stories high, it had a triple arched recessed portico that cast an imposing picture. The apartments in it were huge, consisting of nine to twelve rooms. Paula had heard that it had the toughest co-op board in the city, and purchasers were required to have all cash. She remembered telling her Johnny about Sutton Place then.

"Where do you get these ideas, Paula?" her father would ask with that bemused smile of his. "We're working-class people," he'd say.

"Not the Marasco side," she would remind him.

"Maybe those snob genes of theirs are acting up as I get older." And now she was going to live there, too.

"Well, whaddya know," John announced when he and Rose came to visit them in their new apartment. "I'm proud of you, sweetheart."

Paula responded, "I wish I could feel that for JB now." These days she couldn't help worrying about her son. He seemed to be floundering. He had his own studio apartment in Edison, New Jersey, where he was selling pianos part-time and taking some college courses. She wanted to send him to a first-rate music school to pursue his interest in music, but he refused to go. He lacked confidence in his own ability and talents. Paula admired the fact that her father was the only one who seemed to know what his purpose was in life.

"I don't understand all this talk about being lost," he'd say to his daughter. "The way I learned it, you have a life to live. You get a job, you get married, you raise kids, you do the best you can with what you've got. What's so hard to figure out?" It was clear to John that his job now was to take care of his Rose. He was indefatigable when it came to that. He was also tireless about checking in on both his daughters and inviting them over to dinner.

"Hi, Honey, how's it going for you in the city?" pretty much started every phone call he made to Paula.

Happily, she had good things to report. "Dad, so far so good. We've had our hands full unpacking, but we're having fun. Richard hasn't complained once. I think he's enjoying it here. Every morning he's up early and goes out to buy the papers and brings home hot, fresh bagels."

"Great, Honey, maybe the city will do him some good."

"I hope so, Dad, I hope so. Did I mention to you that I met our neighbors next door? They both work, but they have the cutest little dogs I ever saw, two white Maltese. I think Richard's feet are larger than they are (considering his shoe size is fourteen, triple E). They're just adorable. If Richard decides to leave me, I think I'll replace him with a puppy."

"Paula, now you're talking nonsense. He'll come to his senses. By the way, can we expect you this weekend?" John would ask, trying to sound more nonchalant than he felt.

His daughter hated to disappoint him, but there was so much going on in their lives now. "Dad, do you mind if we pass this weekend, and come out next weekend instead? We've still got loads to do, and furniture is being delivered."

"That'll be fine, kiddo, looking forward to seeing the new city gal."

"You're the best, Daddy."

"You make it easy, Honey. I love you."

Not only was Paula happily enrolled in design school, she was in her glory decorating their new apartment. One thing she was certain; the color white was out for city living. Manhattan had too many incinerators and automobiles. When you opened a window, black soot flew in. No, she wanted their apartment to be warm and inviting. For the city lighting, she was partial to a warm pinky-beige color on the walls. She used that color in most of the rooms. With the patina of warm woods and rich fabrics, she selected a floral wool area rug that had a profusion of colors in shades of red and pinks on a black background. It looked divine and very English on the walnut parquet flooring. The colors in the rug would certainly hide the dirt that would be tracked in from the city streets.

When she would make comments like this to Richard, he'd shake his head and say, "You're nuts, but at least you're pretty nuts." She dragged him to showrooms and antique shops all over town and introduced him to the world of auction houses. He happily accompanied her to Christie's and Sotheby's, where he was impressed when he saw Jack Nicholson and John McEnroe previewing modern art before the auction began. Soon he got into this new world, saying, "Yeah, I see what you mean, quite a learning experience."

The second bedroom in the apartment would do double duty as an office for Richard and a guest bedroom. Paula had taken the rolltop desk from the ranch, his worn cordovan leather chair, his collection of books, and his artwork. In lieu of a bed, she purchased a pull-out sofa, and had the walls painted a warm gray that matched the striped fabric of the sofa. An antique Oushak oriental rug on the hardwood floor gave this postwar apartment an air of old respectability one might expect to find on Sutton Place.

They were pretty much settled into their new apartment when one late afternoon Paula arrived home after a tiring session in her drafting class. She was ready to couch-potato it for the night. Richard helped his wife off with her coat, took her books, and handed her a glass of wine. He looked like the cat that'd just swallowed the canary.

"What's up, Huggy Bear," she said as she quickly licked her lips to savor the chilled white wine he served her.

"I just got off the phone with an old contact from the sporting goods industry. They want me to consult for them."

"Richard, that's wonderful!"

He beamed the happiest smile. "Yep, I start in two days." As it turned out, Richard negotiated a lucrative consulting contract that lasted three years. The power of prayer must have been working for Paula, because the man she fell in love with was resurfacing once again.

While Paula's and Richard's life was improving, her father's days were getting worse. Sensing that her father needed her more, the weekends were becoming predictable for them. Every Saturday morning like clockwork they would drive to New Jersey with dirty laundry in tow. For some reason, Paula preferred her parents' laundry room rather than the building's that all the maids used. "See, you're nuts," Richard would say, hoisting the laundry bag into the car.

John couldn't wait to see them, and eventually the guest room bedroom became their permanent weekend domain. Richard didn't understand why they had to schlep out there every weekend, but Paula did. One day he slipped and said,

"I see only wasted lives, coming out here every weekend, Paula." Quietly she thought to herself, wait, just wait . . . someday you'll be old and I wonder if your children will be there for you. As her mother used to say, "What goes around, come around."

"Richard, I have to do this now. It means a lot to my parents. You don't have to come out with me on the weekends." But he did, he always did. It really wasn't a hardship; her parents welcomed them with big hugs and open arms. John would either cook something special, or if possible they would all venture out to their favorite Chinese restaurant. On the Saturday nights that Rose felt too ill to venture out, they would stay at home. Since Paula liked to cook, she would always try making something special for her father. While the food was in the oven she would turn on the stereo. A home should feel alive, cheerful. With a Perry Como song playing in the background, she took her father's hand. "Come on John Boy, let's dance." Although, he only knew the fox-trot, he was very adept with just those two steps. With his head held high and that twinkle in his eyes, he would twirl Paula around the floor. Another of their favorite tunes was "The Best of Times" by Jerry Herman. Little did they both realize, as they laughed and danced together, these were their best of times.

Rose would sit in her favorite chair watching them, rubbing her arthritic hands, with the pain now escalating to her back. During dinner, enjoying a glass of wine or two, their conversations always looked back and not ahead. "Dad, where did Grandma and Grandpa come from? How old were they when they met? How did they meet?" It became a ritual; Richard started taking notes, mapping out the family tree. They looked through old papers discolored by age marks:

marriage licenses, citizenship papers, baptismal records, newspaper clippings, and family pictures, all handed down from John's dearly departed mother, Angelina.

"Paula, I wonder if I'll ever truly get to Italy? I thought when I retired that Mom and I would do so much traveling." She could hear the remorse in her father's voice.

"Daddy, you will, you will, I know you will." Later that evening in bed, his comments troubled her. How she wished she could take him to Italy right now . . . she could feel the pain of her father's lot in life. Hell, why wasn't he more selfish? Other husbands would take trips in a heartbeat. No, not her father; he was a dinosaur, an extinct species. They don't make men like that anymore. She fell asleep with a great sense of remorse and sadness for her father.

Chapter 26

ONLY IN
NEW YORK

D IVIDING THEIR TIME BETWEEN THE CITY and
the country made Paula and Richard feel like die-hard
New Yorkers. Andrea's boyfriend, Nelson, would kid them,
saying, "There's got to be something wrong with a city when
so many residents leave it every weekend."

City residents like going to where the grass is greener,
or in fact where there's grass at all. Every weekend when
the weather was nice there seemed to be a mass exodus to
either the Hamptons, Berkshires, or, in Paula's case, New
Jersey. The invariable treks among New Yorkers would take
place like clockwork when everyone would converge in the
building's garage.

The protocol was always the same. A resident had to call
ahead so the attendant could get his or her car. As soon
as Paula and Richard stepped off the elevator and out the
front door of the lobby, there it would be, waiting for them.
Some residents never tipped, but Richard always did, which

is another expected ritual of living in Manhattan. Living in a vertical space, you get accustomed to tipping doormen, valet parkers, attendants of all kinds; especially at Christmas when tips become a significant amount of their annual income.

When Paula arrived in the lobby to their waiting car, she would feel like a million bucks. It was part of a dream come true, like Loretta Young sweeping into a room, looking and feeling stylish and elegant. "I love living here, Richard," she would remark.

"Yeah, just like Brooklyn," he'd quip as he stopped to thank the attendant. They were both enjoying this new lifestyle and each other. She was learning a lot as an interior design student, and his consulting work was both lucrative and satisfying for him. One weekend in Jersey, Paula found Richard's explanation of his work to her father rather amusing. "I advise business owners about the strategic and tactical changes that they should consider to improve their revenues and profits."

John told his daughter later that he was glad he asked. "I don't know what that means, but it sure sounds important for business."

The changes in their domestic life were certainly improving their marital relationship.

John said, "I can't tell you how happy that makes me, sweetheart. You know, contrary to what people think, marriages aren't made in heaven. It takes patience, determination, and the ability to see that events change with the passing of time. Remember how devastated you were when Tom passed away?"

"Yes, Dad, and thank God I had you and Mom to care for me."

"True, but you had yourself first. There is an old saying, 'Whether you believe you can or you believe you can't, either way you're right.'"

"Turning into a philosopher, huh, Dad?"

"No, just repeating what an old Greek friend taught me when I was in the service. George, hell of nice guy, grew up in the Lower East side. By the way, are you coming out this weekend? I'm making my famous meatloaf."

"Gee, Dad, JB called earlier in the day and wants to bring over a young lady he's been dating this Saturday evening. I told him yes, and then we're going across the street for dinner at Picasso's for lobsters."

"No problem, I can make the meatloaf on Sunday instead."

"Great, see you and Mom on Sunday." There was no getting around it. Paula had a standing invitation, and it was difficult to say "I can't" to her Johnny.

Nina Lombardi was six years older than Paula's son. She was tall, with jet-black hair that fell over her shoulders. Her features were sharp and angular, and there was something striking about her in an odd way. Paula wondered why her son was attracted to her, and the age difference was a bit of a concern. Their first encounter was pleasant, but she couldn't help but feel a little uneasy when this girl walked into the foyer of their apartment. She had brought a bouquet of flowers, handed them rather brusquely to Paula, and settled into a club chair. There was something different about this young woman, but Paula couldn't put her finger on it. She did notice that Nina was wearing all black. JB was very talkative and, after a glass of wine, the conversation was picking up as Nina started to feel more relaxed as she spoke to JB's parents. Paula learned that she had grown up on Long Island. Her mother was divorced, and she had two brothers and a sister.

When Paula inquired how she had met her son, they both responded simultaneously, "At a bar." Apparently, they had struck up a conversation, one thing led to another, and now they were an item.

When Paula went into the kitchen to freshen the cheese platter, JB quickly followed her. "Well, Mom, what do you think? Isn't she something?"

"Honey, I hardly know her. Give me time to form an opinion."

"OK Mom, just one thing, I think I should tell you that Nina only wears black, and we are thinking of moving in together."

"You mean she never wears colors?" Paula asked, and then the second part of his sentence registered, and before she could say anything, he stated, "Yeh, it's a New York thing, black is cool."

"A New York thing . . . back up, I'm more concerned about the two of you living together." She didn't want to seem rude, but she knew this conversation needed to be continued at a later time. During the conversation at dinner, Paula learned that Nina worked for a marketing company, lived alone, and her pets were a black cat and a tarantula. Apparently her son fit into this picture. Then it dawned on her that Nina reminded her of Morticia on the TV show, *The Adams Family*.

"Richard, what did you think of this girl JB brought over?"

"Well, from the tone of your voice, you have some reservations. Face it, Paula, you'd wonder why your son was attracted to Miss America if he brought her home."

"Richard, don't be ridiculous. Something doesn't sit well with me, but I can't explain why." With so much going on in their life presently, Paula didn't really want to dwell on her son's new relationship. Maybe it would run its course and they would split, as she secretly hoped. In any event, her parents were celebrating their fiftieth wedding anniversary, and she was planning a small dinner party for them.

"Richard, do you realize that we'll probably never make fifty years like my parents?" As she did the math, she cringed at the thought of it.

"Don't think you could handle me for that long?"

"No, I don't, they would have to canonize me if I did."

The dinner party was a simple celebration to commemorate five decades of love. Paula selected the same restaurant where they had held her father's birthday party. This time it was just the family, plus she invited her parents' best man and matron of honor. JB asked if he could bring Nina, and reluctantly she said, "Sure," knowing that Nina would be wearing black from head to toe.

It was endearing for both Paula and Marian to see their parents and their best friends talk about how long they had known each other. As they frequently told the story, after John started dating Rose, Frank (Italo) felt abandoned. John asked Rose if she had a girlfriend to fix up with Frank. Rose immediately suggested her friend Jeanette. It was a successful match, and now both couples were married fifty years and had two adult children in each family, daughters for Rose and John, and sons for the Freccias. They ate well, reminisced about the years gone, and commented that unlike most of their friends, they had the best children.

Chapter 27

THE DIAGNOSIS

"ROSIE, IT'S YOUR GRANDSON, how are you feeling these days?"

"JB, I know you're my grandson. It's my body, not my mind, that's going. It's been a while since you called me."

"Apologies, Rosie. I lose track of time."

"I miss you, JB. Now that you have a girlfriend, we hardly see you anymore. Are you coming over for Christmas?"

"You're a mind reader. That's why I'm calling. I told Nina all about our Christmas Eves. How special they are and, uh, I was wondering if I could bring her with me, if that's okay with you and Grandpa?"

"Well, dear, that's fine with me. You must be pretty interested in this young lady." "Don't tell Mom, but I think she's the one."

"The one what, dear?" Rose knew exactly what was going on with her family at all times. She didn't think that at the tender age of twenty-three JB was old enough or mature enough to even consider marriage. "He needs more time to find himself," she would tell her daughter. "You need to be patient with him." JB held a special place in his grandmother's heart, whereas John could be critical of his grandson and actively voice his disappointment in the choices he was making for himself, Rose would always come to JB's defense. She wouldn't dream of saying no to his request. Seeing him and celebrating Christmas together were more important than any girl. "JB, just tell your mother your plans. She and Grandpa will be doing most of the cooking this Christmas. My parts are wearing out."

"Again with the parts, Rosie? You're not a car."

To Paula's disappointment, JB had moved in with Nina. She didn't quite understand this relationship, and figured with Nina's long black hair, fair complexion, and pointed chin, she looked like a Gothic heroine. It fit the music her son was now composing and playing with his band, The New Creatures. Nina was dark, haunting, and mysterious. Perhaps this was the allure that she held over her son. Was she his muse, his inspiration? Or was this a phase for both of them?

"Paula, she's crazy about him," Richard would remind her. "And maybe she's great in bed," he'd add, with a laugh that cackled.

"Don't say that!" she reprimanded him. "It's my son!"

"But he isn't a kid, Paula."

Then, unexpectedly, the family had far more serious things to think about. It was just one week before Christmas when Rose woke up in excruciating pain. John was beside himself and phoned his daughter. "Paula, Mom is crying and she's in such terrible pain. What should I do?"

Paula could hear her mother in the background, "Babe, babe, help me, help me please."

"Dad, call the doctor and try to get her over to the emergency room. I'll drive out now." As she hung up, she could barely place the phone back into the receiver. Her body felt jittery, her heart was racing. What now, she thought.

Thankfully, the hospital was close by, and while Rose was in the emergency room, her doctor ordered several tests, including a CAT scan. When the results came back, the news was revealed. They found a lung mass on her lower left lobe. Rose was diagnosed with lung cancer. But even more surprising was how she reacted to the news. It was almost as if she felt relief. Now her many years of pain and hurting had a name, lung cancer. She would start chemotherapy right after the holidays. In the meantime, the doctor prescribed medication to ease her pain and help her sleep.

Devastating news hits you in the pit of your stomach, yet life has to go on. With Christmas Eve just a few days away, Paula was determined that cancer would not rob her family of this precious occasion together. Their traditional Italian Christmas would be more meaningful this year, with more food, more decorations, more presents, and anything to hold on to life and their family ritual. John was relieved that his eldest daughter was taking control of the situation, including the Christmas menu. Rose was on enough pain medication to be generally comfortable. She observed her family as they hauled in Christmas lights and polished candlesticks and silverware. She watched them as they went back and forth to the stores and came home with shopping bags filled with food.

Both John and Paula tried to involve Rose in the holiday festivities as much as they could. She'd smile at all the bustling, nod approvingly as they decorated the Christmas tree, and tasted the sauces they were preparing to make sure they met with her approval. Then she'd fall asleep with an expression of serenity on her thin face, curled up in the pink wingback armchair, her slight body ensconced in a beige velour blanket. Everyone tried to keep the mood upbeat, but privately they were tortured souls, afraid what would come next.

On New Year's Eve, Paula cooked an early dinner for four. Marian, Wayne, and Laura came over later for coffee and cake. After dessert, John put his wife to bed, while Marian stayed a while longer to fuss with her mother. By midnight John, Richard, and Paula sat in front of the television watching Dick Clark in Times Square, and as soon as the ball came down the phone rang. Paula knew who it was on the other end. In his usual fashion, wherever JB was on New Year's Eve, he would call his mother. "Happy New Year, Mom!"

"Thanks, son, are you having a good time at that party? It sounds noisy!"

"Yeah, it's alright. We might leave early."

"Well, be careful this evening, a lot of drinkers out tonight. I love you dearly."

"Me too, Mom." As she hung up the receiver, she wondered what the New Year would bring. New Year's Eve always made her feel a little edgy.

It didn't start off so terrible after all. Her father called. "I'll be damned Paula, Mom's feeling better since she started chemotherapy. You should see her. Apparently these drugs are helping her arthritis, too."

"Great, Dad, today they have so many wonder drugs. Not like when Tom was diagnosed fifteen years ago. And we'll be coming out again this weekend, so I'll spend some time with Mom." Who was she kidding, she thought when she got off the phone. Would her mother's fate be any different than Tom's? What would happen in a couple of months?

But she had to be upbeat for her father's sake. They were all trying to put on a good face.

"Okay guys, let's take a drive to Atlantic City for the day. How about that, Mom? You feeling up to it? We can stroll on the boardwalk and hit a few casinos." Her mother now had a wheelchair and a handicap sticker, so it was easier for the family to take her anywhere by car. An excursion out was just to pass the time and get her mind off of her illness. Paula was determined to make good on this unwritten commitment. Your parents take care of you when you're young, and you take care of them when they're old. Going non-stop, Paula's head was whirling with plans, what-to-do's, what they might enjoy next.

Planning ahead for the summer months, Paula talked Richard into renting a house on the Jersey Shore at Long Beach Island. It had four bedrooms and a large deck that overlooked the ocean. She felt certain that the sea air would benefit all. Plus, her father would love playing on the beach with Laura, and he could take her swimming in the Atlantic Ocean. It would be just like the summers the family had spent in Seaside Park when Paula was a child. And to make the shore house feel more comfortable, Paula added her own personal touches and rearranged the furniture.

One weekend JB came down alone and announced he had asked Nina to marry him. This did not sit well with Paula. But she had no choice in his decision. The wedding would take place sometime next year, right after the holidays. "Son, you're only twenty-four. She's thirty. Are you sure this is what you want for the rest of your life?"

"Mom, I love her. She's good for me. Anyway wasn't there an age difference between you and Dad?" Paula felt helpless because he was right. But how could she explain to her love-sick son, that in her opinion, women need to marry older men because emotionally men need time to mature. His impending wedding was the topic of conversation many nights that summer.

"You always make things look so pretty," Rose commented one day to her daughter. Paula was arranging some fresh flowers in her bedroom, and as she turned to thank her, before she could get any words out, Rose said, "You know I don't want to leave you or Marian. I love you girls."

"We love you too, Mom," was all Paula could manage to say without shedding tears. She went back to arranging the flowers, and reached into her pocket to get a tissue. For once in her life she didn't know what to say. The private grieving had begun. The summer was fading. And by the time Labor Day arrived John had developed a cold and terrible cough he couldn't shake. Every weekend when Paula saw her father, he seemed to be on another round of antibiotics. "Dad, why are you taking so many antibiotics?" she innocently asked one day.

"Why? Because the doctor said so, that's why."

"You know antibiotics are only good for bacterial infections, not viral."

"Angel, your daughter is playing doctor again," he said in a sing-song manner to his wife.

"Dad, it's just common sense, I love you too much and I hate that you're taking all these pills. You've had this cough for a while now." Their weekly visits proved to Paula that her father's cough was lingering too long. She felt they were so preoccupied with her mother's illness. Was she neglecting her father's state of health? It was then that Paula decided to make an appointment for him with another doctor, someone she had met several years earlier through mutual friends.

"Dad, I'm taking you to a nice Italian doctor for your cough. You'll like Dr. Antonorri." After a thorough exam, the doctor told them that John's cough was due to congestive heart failure. His lung x-ray revealed fluid. The doctor did his best to reassure them, saying, "With the right medications and a low-sodium diet, he'll be fine."

As though he was reading the furrow between Paula's brows, the doctor added, "Don't worry, Paula. Your mother's situation is entirely different. Your father will be fine."

"You see, Dad, I told you it was more than a cold. You silly boy, listen to your daughter. I have your best interests at heart."

"I know you do, sweetheart. I'm sorry that you're spending so much time with your old folks these days."

"John Boy, you and Mom are my life. What would I do without you both? I would just be bugging Richard or JB, and they're fine without me. Just ask them." On the way home they stopped for an ice cream cone, John's treat.

Chapter 28

BEVERLY HILLS
AND DEATH

W HEN PAULA WASN'T WITH HER PARENTS, she would call home several times a day just to check in on everyone. Lately, every time the phone rang in the apartment she would race to answer it. Feeling constantly anxious these days, waiting for the sky to fall seemed to be her general mindset.

One sunny afternoon, the phone rang while she was in the kitchen making a cup of tea. Running into Richard's office, she tripped on a book, grabbed the phone cord, and pulled the receiver off the hook. "Hello, hello, Paula, is that you?" To her delight, it was her cousin Andrea calling from Los Angeles. "Cuz, is that you?" she repeated.

"Yes, Andrea, it's me! I just tripped on a book."

"How are you? I've been so concerned about you. What's going on?" Hearing Andrea's voice almost made Paula cry. Over the years these first cousins talked more. Now every time Andrea came into New York City from Los Angeles for business, or to see her own mother, they made a special attempt to get together. Andrea had a charismatic personality and was genuinely funny and very caring about her younger cousin's well-being. They had forged a close bond and delighted in each other's company. Dancing and laughing, music or not, jokes or not, they made their own music together like silly school girls. And what made the relationship even more enjoyable was that both of their mates got along really well. Andrea's involvement with Nelson Davis, a television producer, was going strong. One of the stories Andrea enjoyed telling was when she told her mother about her new beau, Nelson.

"Mom was about seventy-two years old," Andrea started. "I didn't often talk about who I was dating, but I could tell that Nelson was special. So, when I was in Brooklyn," she continued, "I told my mother I met a nice man."

"Tell me about him," her mom asked.

"Well, he's tall, dark, and handsome."

Her mother quickly responded, "How dark?"

"He's African-American, Mom."

"Well, that's okay," Pause, beat. "You're not planning to marry him, are you?"

Truth be told, anyone who met Nelson adored him, including Andrea's mother, Tessie. Nelson was a true gentleman, well-grounded, articulate, educated, and good looking. And at 6'2," he and Andrea made a dashing couple. Even their personalities complemented each other. While Nelson was calm and easy going, Andrea was a typically emotional Italian, or maybe just typically Maida. After some years together, Nelson realized that Andrea wasn't interested in getting married. Color wasn't the issue. Her decades-long independence was. So they enjoyed a relationship of being each other's best friends, companions, dates, traveling together, and having a seemingly perfect time of it.

"Oh, Andrea, I'm so glad to hear your voice, I've been a little down. I guess I'm worrying too much about Mom these days."

"That's understandable, sweetheart. You do so much for your family. But don't forget to take care of yourself. That's the reason I'm calling. You and Richard need some fun. And I have the perfect solution. I'm inviting you both to my fiftieth birthday party in Beverly Hills. I hope you can come! You're the only cousin I'm inviting."

"Oh, cuz, that would be wonderful! When is it?"

"The first weekend in October. It will be at our favorite restaurant. Nelson arranged to have a private party on the terrace. He's already selected some fabulous wines. We'll be about twenty of us or so. The weather should be balmy and beautiful. And tell Richard, aside from the wine, he'll enjoy sitting next to you-know-who." Andrea was referring to Mrs. Alan Hamel, better known as actress Suzanne Somers. Andrea had met Suzanne's husband decades ago when she was writing a series of commercials in which he starred. They'd remained friends ever since.

"Oh, Andrea, Richard will be tickled. You know what a sucker he is for a pretty blonde. As soon as I hang up, I'll tell Richard to make the reservations."

"Love it, love it, love it," she exclaimed. "I really want you two there. Now, listen to your older cousin, Paula. You take care of yourself, okay? You know what stress does to the body."

Andrea was a firm believer in the mind-body connection and was always reading books on the subject. She was not only Paula's favorite cousin but her spiritual guru as well. After her upbeat telephone conversation, Paula felt lighter already. In fact, every time she spoke to Andrea she felt better. Andrea had that special quality of seeing the positive in every situation. And, above all, Paula was so proud of the life Andrea had carved for herself from Brooklyn to Beverly Hills. That was quite an accomplishment for a girl to do entirely on her own.

Wait until I tell Richard, Paula thought. But first I better check with Dad. "John Boy, guess who just called me? Cousin Andrea. She invited Richard and me to her fiftieth birthday party in Los Angeles."

"Andrea will be fifty years old! Tessie's little girl. Wow, where does the time go?" "Gee, Dad, I'm not that far from being fifty myself, you know."

"Honey, you and Marian will always be my little girls. Don't you think of JB as a little boy?"

"Yeah, Dad, you're right, I do. But can you handle Mom alone for a week or so if we go? I worry about you."

"Sure, Honey, Marian is around. You and Richard go and have a good time. You deserve a vacation. I couldn't ask for a better daughter. I'm one lucky guy to have you as my kid."

"Dad, I'm the lucky one." As she hung up the phone, she could picture her father's face in front of her. Of course, there were lines and jowls that hadn't been there when she was growing up. Now his hair was more gray than black. Perhaps less of it up front, but it was still tightly curled in the back. Her father would walk into his barbershop and say, "Okay, get out the wire clippers. I need a haircut."

Being in Southern California was a blissful experience for Paula. As an extra special treat, Richard booked them into a world class hotel, the Hotel Bel-Air. Nestled on luxurious grounds with pink Spanish-style bungalows, the hotel was said to be a favorite haunt for celebrities. The place looked like paradise, a Garden of Eden. The gardens were filled with bougainvillea, ferns, palm trees, roses, camellias, azaleas, and fruit trees. There was even a pond with white swans. Paula was beginning to feel balanced again, invigorated with the sheer beauty of it all. Andrea and Nelson joined them for lunch the first day they arrived. They laughed and commiserated about the Maida clan. Andrea squeezed her cousin's hand during lunch. "I'm so glad you were able to get away and come to my party this weekend."

"Cuz, you have no idea how glad I am to be here with you, not to mention Richard. He's looking forward to meeting you-know-who." The party was exactly as Andrea had described: trendy and fresh California cuisine, fine wines, interesting people. And yes, she sat Richard next to Suzanne. All of Andrea's friends commented to Paula that they had never met any of her family all these years she'd lived in California.

"Oh, yes," Paula reassured them, "We have lots of little Italian aunts and uncles running around back East." Paula felt alive. It was so nice to laugh, dress up, and have fun for a while. But her parents were never far from her mind. She called home daily, asking "Mom, how are you?"

"Oh, Paula, dear Paula, are you having a good time?" Something in the tone of her mother's voice troubled her.

"Yes, Mom, we're having a wonderful time. The weather is so mild and sunny. But you didn't answer my question, how are you feeling?"

"Very tired, Paula. When are you coming home?"

"We'll be back in two days. We fly into Newark Airport, and we'll come directly there."

"Good, Paula, that's good." The party was over, time to go home. The flight was uneventful, and the plane right on schedule. As soon as they got to the townhouse, Richard paid the cab driver, and Paula rushed upstairs to see her mother.

"Mom, I'm home." Rose was resting, but when she heard her daughter's voice she opened her eyes, a limp smile draped across her face in welcome.

"I'm so happy to see you," she said. She started to lift her arms to hug her daughter as Paula approached her bed, but they fell back down. Paula sat on the side of the bed and kissed her check, holding her hands.

"I missed you, Mom. You have color today in your face."

"Don't lie to an old lady," Rose retorted. "Go find your father. He can't find his way around his own kitchen without you." Paula got that funny feeling in the gut of her stomach again.

The next morning they had to take Rose to the hospital. Richard picked her up and tried to carry her ever so carefully, but it was like carrying a porcelain doll. Rose sighed and cried at every move. He gently tried to slide her into the front seat of the car. Paula noticed that her stomach looked unusually swollen, like she was pregnant. When Paula called Dr. Lewis, her oncologist, he advised her to bring Rose to the hospital, where he would be waiting for them. He'd ordered his patient a private room and some meds to relieve her pain. "Let's keep her here for a while," he said softly.

Living so close to a first-class hospital made it easy for the family to be with Rose frequently. A day later, Rose was starting to get comfortable once again, or so it seemed to her daughters. Marian and Paula would sit with their mother and talk for hours. Marian would stroke her hair or massage Rose's hands and feet. At some point all of them would try to navigate in bed together, watching television. *Golden Girls* was a perennial favorite. Frequently, Rose would doze off, then, when something deemed important crossed her mind, she'd open her eyes and start speaking as though she'd been awake the whole time. "Paula, I have a ham in the refrigerator. Your father loves ham. Make it tonight for him. And I don't like his cough. He's still coughing, you know."

"Mom, I promise I'll make the ham and take care of Daddy's cough. How about if I come back after dinner and stay with you tonight?"

"No, no, you girls go home. I'll see you in the morning, I'll be fine here." The girls were reluctant to leave their mother. As they walked down the hospital corridor, quietly holding each other's hands for emotional support, Paula pushed the down button by the elevator.

Marian turned suddenly to Paula. "I have to kiss Mommy one more time. You don't have to wait for me."

"I'll wait, sis," she answered. That evening, no one really slept well. Paula tossed and turned and at three a.m. went downstairs to the kitchen. Perhaps a warm cup of milk and a Fig Newton cookie would help her sleep. It did, and she awoke three hours later. This time she decided to get dressed and go to the hospital early, but not until after she made a pot of coffee and some toast with orange marmalade. Mom would enjoy that, she thought, so she left a note for her father and Richard, who were both still asleep.

As Paula approached her mother's room, she noticed nurses going in and out. Once inside the room, she saw that two nurses were trying to catheterize their patient. Her mother was thrashing her arms and legs and moaning helplessly.

"Stop it!" Paula yelled.

"She has to void, we have to put the catheter in."

"No, leave her alone, don't touch her." Paula was extremely adamant and angry. Couldn't they see her mother was in pain? She ran over to the bed and pulled the blanket up over her mother's half-naked body.

"Mommy, Mommy, its Paula, I'm here. You don't have to keep fighting, mommy. Don't hang on for our sake. It's okay to leave us. Don't fight, Mommy. You've been through so much. We love you."

With that, the floor resident walked in. "What's wrong?" Paula asked.

"I just spoke to Dr. Lewis; I'm going to give her something to manage her pain. Her heart seems to be failing." As soon as the resident gave her the injection, Rose's body seemed to relax. Whatever he gave her was starting to work.

Knowing that she had to call home immediately, Paula dialed out. Richard answered the phone, "Richard, get Daddy over here fast. Mom has taken a turn for the worse." As soon as she hung up, her sister arrived. "Who phoned you?" she instinctively asked.

"No one, I couldn't sleep. I just came over. What's happened?" Paula had the strange feeling that her mother was waiting for the three of them to arrive.

With that, John walked into the room. With a concerned look on his face, his brows twisted, he went to his wife's bedside and so delicately took his wife into his arms. She was so gaunt and brittle. "Angel, Angel, I love you. You are my life, my world, don't leave me. Angel, don't leave. I'll be with you someday, don't leave me, Angel."

Marian was inconsolable. She was losing her mother and her best friend. Paula was glad that they weren't there earlier to see Rose's discomfort. The morphine was working,

Rose was quieter now, and before long, her heart stopped. It was over. They were all with her. Silence enveloped the room—they wept.

People filed in and out of the funeral home, viewing Rose's body and expressing their condolences. Large wreaths were delivered day after day from family members and dear friends. They exchanged kisses with relatives and thanked them for being there. Then someone would break down, one of John's sisters or Rose's brothers. John was distant and distraught. He was there, but not there. He said all the right things to everyone who hugged him. He heard his praises sung for how much he'd done for his wife and how much she loved him. Then he had watch them approach her casket. He would hear their words as they paused and looked down: "Look how beautiful she looks," "Oh, our beautiful Rose," "Piccata," "How she suffered."

The hard part was yet to come. By the day of the funeral Mass and burial, the three family members clung to each other. How do you say your last good-byes? Choked-back words, unstoppable sobs, "Mommy, I'll take care of Daddy . . . I promise." "Angel, we'll be together again. I love you. I love you." Then Paula's father bent over Rose's casket and kissed her, taking her hand in his. His two sons-in-laws finally guided him away.

Catholic Masses tend to be resplendent, with priests in heavy robes of brocade and elaborate rituals with a cappella singing or a choir filling the large space with the music of Mozart or Bach. Rose would have approved of her last hurrah. Richard gave a poignant eulogy titled "Rosie's Recipe for Life" and made sure he included personal details that included anyone who ever dined at Rose's table.

John had been a wonderful husband for fifty-one years; it was going to be difficult for him without his other half. Paula turned her attention totally to her father in his grief. All she could think about were the sacrifices he'd made for his family. Now it was his turn to enjoy his life. "Paula, I feel so empty. What will I do without your mother?"

"Here's what I think, Daddy. Mommy would want you to enjoy your life now. You took such good care of her for so long." She decided that, as soon as things settled down, she would plan a trip for him. Finally, without feeling guilt or remorse, he would be able to travel and not worry about his beloved wife. She knew that Italy, the birthplace of his adored parents, Angelina and Joseph, would be the first of many trips where they would accompany him. He would like that, Paula thought, and we could even invite his sister Catherine. But for now they would have to deal with this day. But what plans don't take into account is the unexpected.

Chapter 29

♥

A Downward Spiral

It's a tradition in Italian-American families that after a funeral, a big meal is served to the mourners who attended. Death or not, it's time to *mangia*! After the cemetery, the funeral director announced that everyone was invited for lunch at Uncle Mike's Restaurant, a casual Italian bistro up the street from Rose and John's home.

Sure enough, the tables quickly became laden with plates of antipasti, caprese salads, and glasses of red wine accenting the black worn by everyone at the long, rectangular table. Waiters passed baskets of bread, hands reached for butter and bottles of olive oil. The repast had begun. Paula and Richard sat at a table with John and his two sisters Catherine and Tessie. Paula was feeling terribly cold, and was too numb to eat—picking at her food, moving the salmon toward this side, the vegetable over to that side, trying not to be too obvious.

"Paula, you're not eating!" her Aunt Catherine said with a slight rebuke in her voice. "Listen to me. No matter what happens, there are three things we always gotta do: we gotta breathe, we gotta eat, we gotta shit."

"I can't. I'm too upset." For a second, she was too stunned at this seeming insensitivity to say a word. Then, the gist of what she'd said hit home. She could feel her face register total amusement and thought, "What a concept! My mother is dead. All around me people are digging into their bowls of pasta, steaks, and fish. I can hardly move. But sonofagun, my aunt is right." Catherine was a survivor, and her sense of humor served her well over the years. Paula could see how her father developed such a kinship with her. She was one tough cookie, and she certainly had a way with words!

If ever the Maidas had a family crest, she had no doubt what the family motto would be. Paula kissed her aunt and proceeded to try to eat a little. By this time, conversations had become more animated with each toast: To Rose! To Johnny! To Paula! To Marian! The banter was going around the room, "They never left her side." "My brother's a saint." "They brought those girls up right. Look at how they stayed with their mother."

Finally, some hours later, people started filing out. Paula glanced at her Aunt Tessie, all 4'11" inches of her. She was wrapped in a black coat with a scarf around her neck. Topped by her short, gray hair, she looked like a chubby pepper shaker. Sure enough, even today, she was taking a doggie bag home with her. Everyone kissed and made small conversation, with many invitations to "come for dinner," "don't forget we're here," "don't be a stranger now." Then they were gone. John graciously went to the back of the room to settle up the bill.

Marian and Wayne offered to take John home. He looked exhausted, and they thought he should rest a while. JB had indicated to his mother that he wanted to talk to her a minute. Nina had disappeared into the ladies' room. "Mom, can I talk to you?"

"Of course son, is anything wrong?"

"Mom, Nina and I are set to get married in three months. You know that. Do you think that's still okay?"

"JB, to tell you the truth, I wish you weren't getting married at all."

"I know you're not crazy about her, Mom, but I love her. All the arrangements have been finalized."

"Yes, I know."

JB and Nina had planned a small wedding for fifty people. They selected the penthouse at the Beekman Tower Hotel in New York City, and Paula offered to pick up the tab. Aunt Catherine said she was a jackass for doing it.

"Aunt Catherine, I'm not happy about it, believe me. But the first time I met Nina's mother, she made it clear she couldn't afford to contribute to the wedding. Before I knew it, I blurted out that I would help out."

"Was that before or after she took off her coat?" Catherine asked snidely. Paula recounted the meeting with Nina's mother. She invited her to their apartment in the city for dinner, since she wanted to meet her.

Nina's mother had told her in no uncertain terms, "I'm divorced and had to raise the children on my own. It was very difficult for me. He was an abusive husband. But I promise I'll love your son as if he were my own."

Paula felt sorry for the woman, and that's when she offered to pick up the tab for the wedding. It was a decision she would later come to regret. But on this day, the wedding was the farthest thing from her mind. Ever since JB's father died, she found it difficult to refuse her son anything. Call it guilt, call it whatever you want. "Go ahead, son, make your plans." Someone should be happy these days; why not her son, she thought. Sure, the timing was off, but she hoped her son's wedding would lighten their family's grief. Her main concern right now was getting her Johnny back on track. He was a youthful looking seventy-four, albeit a tired one. Why shouldn't he still have good things ahead of him? In fact, Paula suspected that two widowed neighbors had their eyes on her father. They both came to the wake and sent food to the house.

"Dad, Richard is going back to the city to pick up some more clothes for me. I'm going to stay with you for a while."

"Honey, you don't have to do that. Marian is around to help me."

"No way, Dad. We have a lot to take care of, and I'm not letting you do it by yourself. Anyway, Marian has Laura to watch out for." She didn't want to tell him that Marian was taking her mother's death poorly. Her sister found it too painful to go into the house. Walking in the front door, Marian expected to see her mom's face and still longed to have their girlfriend chats. Besides, Marian didn't know what needed to be done.

Paula was with her father only three days when she noticed how bad his coughing had become, and now it was compounded by a shortness of breath. It seemed worse in the morning. He seemed to be choking on his own phlegm. She could hear her mother's words resonate in her head, "Paula, take care of Dad's cough. I don't like it."

"Dad, this is ridiculous. You shouldn't be coughing like this. I'm making an appointment with a pulmonary man." Later that morning, she contacted the pulmonary group that had taken care of her mother. They arranged to see John in two days, expressing sympathy for the family's loss.

"Richard, I'm taking Dad to the doctor tomorrow. Take care of the apartment. Remember to eat. Don't make a mess. And don't forget I love you."

"Paula, your mom made me promise that I would take good care of you, and I will, Honey Bear. Don't worry about a thing. Just take care of your father. I love you, too." Rose was right, it's not how you start out in life, it's how you finish that counts. Paula was grateful that Richard was becoming more of the man she needed, especially now. She needed his empathy and support.

As Paula sat in the doctor's office with her father, she tried to keep the conversation light. "Let's talk about our trip to Italy next spring, Dad. May is such a beautiful time to travel. We could even ask Aunt Catherine if she'd like to join us." It wouldn't be easy to extract Catherine from her beloved home. She'd lived in a little Cape Cod house in Bethpage, Long Island, for decades. The small rooms were carefully arranged and cleaned every day. And then there was her garden, and for a woman who lived alone and couldn't drive, she always kept busy.

"Paula, you're just like me, you like to decorate," she'd often told her niece. Paula didn't have the heart to tell her that their taste levels were worlds apart. Plastic slip covers and crocheted doilies filled her aunt's rooms. John loved her dearly. For him, Paula had a hunch Catherine would actually leave home.

Before long, the nurse came out, "Mr. Maida, the doctor will see you now." Both sat in the doctor's office explaining the events, the coughing, and all the antibiotics he'd taken, his present medication of a diuretic and Procardia. Paula gave the doctor her father's past chest x-rays. He put them up to the lighted screen. Minutes ticked by. He seemed to be studying them intensely, his finger pointing here, there. He said nothing. Father and daughter looked at each other with a quizzical stare. Paula broke the silence.

"His other physicians said it was a bad cold, and Dr. Antonorri said it was congestive heart failure."

"Some doctors might say that, but I wouldn't."

"What are you saying?" John asked nervously. "Is it lung cancer?"

"It could be, Mr. Maida," was the doctor's reply. A bomb had just dropped in the room. Paula's head felt like it had just exploded. She wanted to fall on the floor.

"Oh, God, dear God, what did he just say?"

Her father looked the doctor straight in the eye. "Last week I buried my wife from lung cancer. Are you saying a week later I have the same thing? Am I going to die now, too?"

"Mr. Maida, we need to do some testing. I want to get a sample of the fluid from your lungs. Let's just wait and see. In the meantime, let me examine you."

Paula left the room. She felt cold, hot, her body was shaking. She called Richard. "Richard, Richard, I'm in the doctor's office with Dad. He thinks my father has lung cancer."

Silence. "Richard, are you still there?"

"Paula, it can't be true. I'll drive to New Jersey and meet you at home."

Tests. Samples. A first opinion. A second opinion. The diagnosis couldn't be worse. Paula accompanied her father to the hospital, where they removed one-and-a half quarts of

fluid from his lungs. He was literally drowning. The report
came back: non-small cell lung cancer that had metastasized
outside of the pleura cavity.

She asked the doctor privately, "What would you do if
it was your father?"

His answer, "Honestly, take him home."

All the things that were important in her life were slip-
ping away. If she felt this way, she couldn't imagine what her
father was feeling. He was a dead man walking.

The decision was made; Paula would not allow her father
to live by himself now. She spoke with Richard, and he was
supportive of his wife's decision to care for her father in
New Jersey. He would go back into the city and come out on
weekends. Rose had died on October 17, and in two months
there would be another Christmas season upon them. But
this time it would be the last for John, the last for his daughters to have a parent. The doctors made it perfectly clear that
John's condition was terminal. Sure, they could start chemo,
but in their opinion, his cancer was too advanced.

The holidays, which once held so much excitement and
joy for the family, became an exercise in false bravado.
Paula wanted to go back in time. That comfortable feeling of security, knowing her parents would always be there
for her. Instead, she felt stripped, naked, with raw emotions
ready to attack anyone in her way. The weather also increased
her anxiety. November was bitterly cold, with severe snow
storms. All you could do was stay inside and hibernate. Her
father played the hand he'd been dealt. Mostly, he wanted
to talk.

"Paula, I don't want to be a burden on you. I don't want
you to go through what I did with my father. It's not digni-
fied. You shouldn't see these things."

"Dad, you worry too much. It won't be like that. Don't think so much. Let's just enjoy today." God only knew what he was thinking; he knew his cancer was too advanced. The mental anguish, the hours of anxious voices racing in his head. Paula made sure he had anti-depressants and sleeping aids. Her main objective was to make this time more tolerable for him.

They cooked together and drank wine. Even a simple meal like sausage and broccoli rabe and a loaf of hot, crusty Italian bread was special. Father and daughter talked for hours about his boyhood days in Brooklyn, his siblings, his beloved parents, the Italy he would never get to visit, his days in England during the war. He even divulged that he had sex with an English girl.

He had broached the subject with great hesitation; he lowered his eyes, and his voice. "Paula, there's something I want to get off my chest. I never told anyone." Paula wasn't all that convinced it was anything she wanted to hear, but he blurted out his secret. "No, I never told your mother." Just mentioning her filled his twisted face with grief.

"Dad, those were different times. No one would judge you for that. You were two young people who found comfort in each other."

Paula found it ironic that both of her parents would eventually share their secrets with her. It was a single indiscretion that they'd each had during war times, as if they'd committed a serious crime. It must have bothered both of them all these years. How unfortunate, she thought, to be weighed down by such an insignificant encounter by today's standards.

There were many days when strong emotions came to the surface, especially when John was consumed with bleak thoughts. She could read her father's face, the wandering lost look he held in his eyes. She could only distract him for short periods of time, so that's when she decided to rent foreign films for them to watch after dinner, mostly Italian with subtitles. But John's two favorite films were in French: *Jean de Florette* and *Manon of the Spring*, starring Gerard Depardieu. It was during one of those films that Paula got up from the living room sofa to get a drink in the kitchen.

As she did so, her father grabbed her hand, and ever so gently he kissed the top of it. "Paula, thank you for being here with me and for taking care of me." She could feel her eyes getting wet. He was breaking her heart. She couldn't fix him. She couldn't change his fate. He was going to die on her. She was losing her Johnny. Damn this disease.

"Don't be silly, John Boy. Can I get you an ice cream sandwich?"

Everyone, especially relatives and friends, seemed confused and awkward when they were informed of John's illness. At first, people called when they heard the news, but now the phone was ringing less these days. Paula understood, but it was harder for her father to comprehend. With each passing day, John was getting more attached to his daughter. He became her shadow.

"Dad, I'm going to Loehmann's to look for a dress for JB's wedding."

"Can I come with you?"

"Sure, Dad, we can have lunch out, too!"

The weather in December was just as bad as the previous month, and to ease the monotony for her father Paula invited family members and friends to come over for dinner. For once she was happy that Tony was coming over; he was aware of the dire situation his uncle was in. When John excused himself to the bathroom, Paula asked Tony if he was planning to attend JB's wedding.

"Of course, I am."

"Great, can I ask you to keep an eye on dad for me that evening?"

"Gee, Paula, I'm looking forward to having a good time myself," was his reply.

So much for the ties that bind.

That last Christmas together, Paula and Marian decorated the rooms so they looked cheerful. Pictures of their mother were scattered about with red ribbons, and a small tree sat in the corner of the living room. John and Paula once again planned the Christmas Eve menu. This year Richard's daughters, Mara and Anny, wanted to be with the family. John had become like a grandfather to them, and they were serious seafood eaters. Christmas Eve supper included baked clams, *scungilli* salad, shrimp scampi, fried scallops, and linguini with mussels in red sauce. Marian found her mother's recipe for *struffoli* and *zeppoli*. And to everyone's surprise, Marian's first-time attempt to make *struffoli* was outstanding—Paula figured it must be in the genes, since both women loved their desserts.

John had little Laura to hug and kiss that evening, and he got a kick out of watching her open her presents. JB and Nina came with loads of perfectly wrapped gifts (Nina's specialty), impeccable and adorned with handmade ornaments. They managed to make the best of this sad and sweet "happy-to-be-together; please-God-help-us" Christmas.

January was an exceptionally bone-chilling month, with temperatures dipping to record lows. One morning, John noticed blood on his pajama bottoms.

"Dad, it's probably just a kidney stone you passed," Paula said, hoping to sound casual. Another morning, his neck was swollen. He'd started radiation treatments. By this time he was losing several pounds a week, so everyone insisted he eat more pasta and ice cream. Sleep did not come easy to John.

On a cold morning with wind chills in the single digits, John walked into the bedroom where his daughter slept. "Paula, I can't sleep."

"What's wrong, Dad?"

"I'm afraid," he apologetically whispered.

"Dad, hop in bed with me." His body was shaking. She rubbed his shoulders, looking at the back of his head and his white curly hair. This was her father, her strong father, the hero of her youth. Even the strong end up like this, she thought bitterly. "Rest, Dad, get some rest. I'm with you."

The following week, John was admitted into the hospital. Too many sweets and carbs had elevated his sugar levels. He was now a diabetic. Suffering from extreme fatigue, he was also diagnosed as being anemic. In a few days under medication, his glucose was under control. And with a blood transfusion, his chipmunk cheeks looked rosy once again. "Hi Dad, you're looking good today."

"Tony came to visit me, Paula. And I called up my sister Catherine. It's her birthday today. You should telephone her when you get home."

"Will do. You know your grandson will be getting married in a few days. Do you think you'll be up to going to the wedding?"

"Honey, the only way I won't be there is if I'm in a box." Marian came into the room with Laura, which immediately put a smile on his face. Later, Richard arrived, and the two men watched football for a while. Finally, after so many visitors, John said, "Okay, you kids go home. I'm tired now."

"Goodnight, Dad." Each of them kissed and touched him. Paula squeezed her father's hand and patted his head, something she did often these days; it was 8:15 p.m. At 1:30 a.m., the phone rang. The physician on call introduced himself and then told Paula that her father had passed away in his sleep.

Paula later learned from her cousin Tony that the day before he died, John told him in conversation, "Tomorrow Aunt Rose will be dead three months. I hope she comes for me." Apparently, he got his wish. Three months to the day—his Angel came for him!

Chapter 30

HEAVEN AND
HELL ON EARTH

O N THE SAME MORNING THAT PAULA'S FATHER
passed away at 4:30 a.m., Pacific Standard Time, Los
Angeles experienced the most damaging earthquake since
the great San Francisco earthquake of 1906. It registered
6.7 on the Richter scale. People died, and thousands were
seriously injured.

Paula was hoping to talk to Andrea to tell her that her
father had died, and now she was also concerned for her
cousin's safety. All the phone lines were out; hour after hour
she tried in vain to reach her. In a few days Andrea and
Nelson were scheduled to fly to New York to attend JB's
wedding, but she needed to speak to her now. They finally
connected the next morning.

"Paula, I'm okay. I just spoke to my mother, and she told
me about Uncle John. Oh, sweetheart, I'm so sorry for you. I
wish I could do something to ease your pain. I wish I could
wrap my arms around you and give you a big hug."

"Andrea, I was so worried about you. I'm losing everyone I love. I feel so numb inside, and it's so damn cold. It's like Siberia here. The wake is tomorrow and the funeral the day after. Make sure you pack your boots and warm clothing."

Under the existing circumstances, Paula was sorry that she didn't insist on the wedding being postponed. Now it was too late. The day of the funeral the temperature was eleven degrees and the wind chill minus seventeen. Driving was treacherous. There were icy patches on the roads, and tree branches hung low, covered with icicles. Just the immediate family and a dozen or so close friends and relatives who could brave the roads attended the funeral. Paula's Uncle Ernie, cousins Robert and Tony, along with Tony's buddy Jerry, showed up. John's sisters lived too far away, and with the disruptive snow and Arctic air mass, it was too dangerous for them to venture out.

It was a horrible day that only got worse. Due to the extreme weather, the funeral home lost electricity. The church was cold inside, no lights, and no organ music. The hearse carrying John's coffin skidded on ice. Aside from Richard's eloquent eulogy for his father-in-law, everything else seemed to be going wrong. Paula wondered what adversity would befall them next. Apparently, God had abandoned her family, and now Mother Nature was angry, too! Or was all this misery an outward demonstration of what they felt like inside?

After the service and short drive to the gravesite, once again they went to Uncle Mike's Restaurant for the repast. At Rose's luncheon, people had been more social, lingered, and were more talkative. Now, just three months later, the few people who did stay were careful of what they said. Everyone seemed stunned at how quickly John had died after his wife. Soft murmurs, hushed tones, people ate quietly and departed quickly to get back on the icy roads before weather conditions grew worse and the sun went down.

"Marian, are you and Wayne coming back to the house?" Paula asked.

"No, I don't think so. Laura's tired, and I'm drained."

"I know how you feel, me, too. I think Tony and his friend are coming back to . . ." she stopped herself. To where? Nobody lived there anymore.

"Oh, hell, you're tired, Paula."

"It's okay, they won't stay too long. By the way, can you drop JB and Nina at the train station? They're going back into the city."

"Sure. Talk to you later."

When the small group arrived back at the townhouse, the rooms looked dark and bleak: no father and no mother. Paula turned on the gas fireplace and excused herself to go upstairs to put on some comfortable clothing. She changed into comfy worn blue jeans, a warm sweater, and wool socks.

"Do you want a cup of coffee?" she asked half-heartedly.

"How about a glass of wine?" Tony replied. It was about three in the afternoon. Richard, Tony, and his friend started drinking. Paula put out some snacks. The hours passed, and the three men seated at her parents' dining room table seemed to have an insatiable thirst that afternoon. It was almost time for dinner. Could she let them drive home on an empty stomach? The phone rang. It was Marian. Paula told her they were still there.

"Are you serious?" Marian said in a surprised tone of voice.

"Yup, I'm exhausted. I'll give them something to eat and send them home."

"Have they been drinking?"

"What do you think?"

Since Paula hadn't gone food shopping in days, she checked the refrigerator and freezer. She found frozen gravy with meatballs and a loaf of Italian bread wrapped in foil. Great, she thought. I just need to boil some water for the spaghetti, and defrost the gravy, that should satisfy them. Then she prepared the food, set the table, and plated the pasta. After supper, she cleared the table. One of the men asked for a cup of espresso. No one offered to help. They just gave her orders like she was their waitress.

As she stood in the kitchen, it dawned upon Paula that the meal she had just served was thanks to her father. She had just fed them her father's last meatballs. He was dead in his grave, and those three inconsiderate men who were half-tanked from all the wine they consumed had enjoyed a meal prepared by her Johnny. She looked up through the kitchen cutout into the dining room and saw them laughing, drinking.

Then something happened to her—she snapped! Blood rushed to her head. She loathed them. The very sight of them disgusted her. Her Johnny was dead. The man she could lean on for anything and everything was gone forever. How dare they get drunk and laugh and tell their stupid jokes while she served them like a goddamned maid. She started screaming at them. "Get out of my father's house! Get out of here, all of you!" She threw the microwave on the ceramic floor, breaking several tiles. Every dish and glass she could get her hands on went flying.

She must have scared the living daylights out of them, because in a flash, they were gone. Paula didn't recall what happened. She found herself sitting on the cold tile floor crying and crying: crying for her father; crying for her mother; crying for her overwhelming loss. "How could this happen? I'm so alone, alone, alone." She had no idea how long she sat on that floor, rocking back and forth, and tears streaming down her face. "Mommy!" "Daddy!" At some point she became aware of the doorbell ringing repeatedly, and she heard pounding on the door. Picking herself up, she saw yellow lights reflected in the living room glass window. There was an emergency vehicle outside; two men were at the door.

When she opened the door, they came in and asked if she was all right. She was speechless. Later, Paula found out that her dear cousin suggested to Richard that he thought she was having a nervous breakdown, and suggested he call 911.

"Don't go back there, Richard. Remember what happened to that guy, Bobbitt; his wife cut off his penis when he was asleep" Tony warned, apparently in all seriousness.

Paula was drying her eyes with a dish cloth, trying to think of what she could say to the two paramedics standing in front of her, when her sister rushed into the house.

"This is my sister, don't take her away. We just lost both of our parents. We buried my father today. She's just upset; I'll stay with her tonight." Marian had come to her sister's rescue. Paula put her head on her shoulder and started crying again. When things calmed down, Marian told Paula that Richard had gone back into the city to stay at their apartment. Under the circumstances, he thought that was a safer place to be.

After a glass of brandy to settle her nerves, Paula told Marian, "At least I got them out of the house."

"Yeah, but did you have to make such a mess?"

The two sisters, on their hands and knees, cleaned up the mess in the kitchen. Even in a crisis, good Italian girls clean. When they finally got to bed that night, they just hugged each other and talked. It finally hit them; it was just the two of them. That's all they had left, each other.

Chapter 31

RECOVERY—
PHASE I

T HERE WAS NO TIME TO GRIEVE. In less than five
days, Paula's son was getting married. She never did get
a chance to buy a new dress for the wedding. Instead she
found a black wool cocktail suit trimmed in black velvet in
the back of her closet in the city apartment. She just had to
move a button on the skirt so it would sit at her waist and
not fall down. When she mentioned that to Andrea, her
cousin joked, "I hate thin people. You could eat a cow and
you wouldn't gain weight. I eat a shred of spinach and I'm
up a pound."

Andrea liked to exaggerate.

Cousin Tony was a no-show at the wedding and hadn't
called. He was just absent. Paula gathered that the scene
in the kitchen had been enough to keep him far, far away.
Richard and Paula eventually made up.

"Gee, Honey Bear," he said, forlornly. "I had no idea how
upset you were that evening."

"Excuse me!" she said sharply. "My mother died and three months later my father dies! I feel like an orphan! And you have no idea??!! How could you be so oblivious to my feelings?"

"Uh, gee, yeah . . ." Lord knows, emotions confused him.

Andrea would often say, "Paula, don't you get it? Men are simple creatures. They want food, sex, work, and sleep. We want love, understanding, compassion, constant attention, and rarely know who scored the last touchdown." Maybe Andrea was right, she thought. Being sensitive to other people's feelings was a skill Richard found difficult to acquire. Besides, Paula had to admit she was no picnic to live with; through the eight years of their marriage, they had to deal with a lot of her family's problems along with their own relationship. Above all, Paula loved him, and he still looked irresistible to her in his double-breasted tuxedo.

The Saturday that JB and Nina were wed, the weather behaved. Clear blue skies with remains of snow on the streets adorned the city. The sun was shining, while temperatures remained chilly enough to feel like the iced champagne served at the reception. The art deco inspired penthouse of the Beekman Hotel fit the occasion. Hors d'oeuvres were passed, the bubbly flowed, the DJ played, and dinner was served—all very New York chic. Everyone looked lovingly at the groom as he sat down at the baby grand piano to play a composition that he'd composed for his new wife. Paula was pleased with the bride's appearance. With Nina's jet-black hair softly curled, pink make-up, and a white tulle bridal gown, she looked radiant.

With enough Moet & Chandon to drink, Paula was trying to forget that the people who were most important to her were visibly absent at this black tie affair. She recalled dancing the twist with her niece, Laura, and then watching Andrea and Nelson dancing. "Don't they make an attractive couple, Bear?" she asked her husband.

"Class act," he acknowledged.

"The two of them." Finally, all said farewell to the bride and groom, wishing them a happy lifetime together.

It had been one incredible week. Emotionally and physically, Paula was drained and running on empty. In retrospect, she thought how nice it would be to leave the cold and spend a few days somewhere warm, perhaps Florida. She desperately needed a break to rest and reflect on all that happened, but most of all, she needed time to heal.

Instead of resting, they moved back to New Jersey. Richard made it sound so simple. Since his consulting job had ended and Paula was finished with design school, it made perfect sense to move back into the vacant townhouse. Their lease in New York was coming up for renewal in two months, and paying thousands of dollars a month seemed foolish.

"Marian, Richard and I discussed things, and we decided to move back to Jersey."

"Paula, this makes me so happy! It's so empty without Mommy and Daddy. At least you'll be close by."

"Marian, could you help me sort things? We still have their clothes and all the furniture to deal with."

"Absolutely! I couldn't face doing it alone anyway."

Two months later, after schlepping back and forth from the city to the suburbs, supervising the painters, installing a hardwood floor in the living room and new carpeting throughout, and disposing of her parents furniture to relatives, Paula and Richard moved back to the suburbs. Finally, after weeks of physical activity, Paula could stop and rest. But her mind didn't register that; mentally, she was still on overdrive.

Everyone who has ever loved and lost someone knows the feelings you experience; the inexplicable guilt, rethinking past events over and over, the sleepless nights, nightmares, the daily numbness you feel going about doing mundane chores. To compound the situation, Paula was now becoming a hypochondriac and cancer phobic. It wasn't so much the days that she dreaded but the nights. She couldn't sleep; her mind would conjure up ugly visions. She was waking up with palpitations and in a cold sweat. Was she having a heart attack? Was it cancer? She would get up, go downstairs, and sit in the darkness for hours crying. She knew it was time to see Dr. Kross.

"Look, Paula, what you've gone through is bound to have psychological effects on you. All of your tests have come back negative. You don't have cancer. I can prescribe something to help you temporarily."

"Thank you. You've been very reassuring. I'll take a prescription, but I'm not sure if I'll use it."

Early one morning, after another sleepless night, Paula was perusing the local paper. An item in the classified section caught her eye. It read, "Seven-week male Maltese puppy for sale." Her fingers were dialing the telephone number before she realized what she was doing. She made an appointment with the owner to see the pup that afternoon, and a smile came across her face.

Richard came into the kitchen for a cup of coffee. "Boy, coffee smells good. Any orange juice left?"

"No, only cranberry juice. Guess what I'm doing today?"

After she told him her plans, with a look of utter amazement, he said, "You want a dog now? After everything you've been through, a dog?"

"Why not? Don't you remember how adorable our neighbor's dogs were in the city? They're such cute little things. Anyway, I'm just going to look at him."

As soon as Paula rang the bell and entered the vestibule of the house, her eyes glanced down, and she noticed a tiny little puppy on the wood floor. Wherever she walked, he seemed to follow the red sneakers she was wearing. It was love at first sight. How could anyone resist a three-pound white fluffy snowball? The next day, after Paula purchased all the items needed for a new puppy, she picked him up and brought him home. As soon as she opened the garage door leading to the kitchen, without hesitation the new pup walked into his crate. Her decorating skills now reflected in the dog crate; she placed a leopard throw and a little pillow inside it. The pup made himself comfortable, as if to say, "I'm home." The first night, he was so quiet, Paula checked on him several times just to make sure he was alive and still there.

After two weeks, Paula announced to friends and family that after much soul searching, she thought she made the best decision. "It was either Prozac or a puppy, and this little fella is making me happy," she told her friend Joe Day. She hadn't seen Joe in a while, since his new position at the Waldorf Astoria was keeping him in the city. But he did have time to visit a psychic. He was talking in his usual rapid-fire way, anxious to tell her about what she had told him.

"Paula, this lady was so good. The things she told me. You really have to go see her. In fact, I'm going to make an appointment for you."

"I'm not into stuff like that, Joe."

"Paula, you're going, even if I have to drive you there myself. It's fun. Think of it as entertainment, and it's my gift to you."

A month later, she went. The woman lived in a pleasantly cluttered house and greeted her warmly. Paula wasn't sure what to expect. She found herself with a nicely attired middle-age woman in slacks and an oversized sweater. Joe assured Paula that he'd told her nothing about her life. As Paula sat in a comfortable armchair, she listened. Most of what she had to say was information that wasn't too significant to Paula. But then Paula sat up straight and began listening more attentively. The woman began to talk about Paula's father.

"I can feel that you're a very emotional woman," she began. "You're hurting and in pain because of a lost one. His name starts with a J." Paula started to cry, and she was handed a tissue. "Paula, don't think your father isn't watching over you. Spirits do try to communicate, but you have to be receptive. They can't speak to you, but they will try to reach you through all of the five senses. It could be through the sense of smell, touch, sound. Just be aware of it." Then she said something Paula focused on, "*Your father can do more for you where he is now than he could do for you on earth. He will be the wind beneath your wings.*" What a touching sentiment, Paula thought. If only it were true. She left feeling better. The woman's words were comforting, if nothing else.

As the weeks went by, Paula kept busy training her pup, who she named after her father—Giovanni Puccini Maida, but called Pucci for short. She contemplated working as an interior designer but couldn't get herself motivated. Her energy level was still low, but fate was working in her favor. An acquaintance in town called one day and asked Paula if she would be interested in working part-time in her antique and consignment shop. It ended up a perfect fit for Paula's time and talents—she decorated the store windows and accepted decorative items and furniture for consignment.

Her days were beginning to feel normal to a small degree. Life had a purpose and a routine—caring for a puppy, working, cooking, and late evening phone calls to her sister. It was an evening ritual that the sisters established soon after John's passing. Every night, their conversation would end talking about their parents. How wonderful they were; how fortunate they were to have them; how empty and awkward they felt without them in their lives.

June was fast approaching, and Paula realized that her sister would be soon be celebrating a milestone birthday. She hated the fact the Marian had to celebrate this day without their parents being there. As the family matriarch now, Paula wanted to recognize her younger sister in a special way. A trip to the shopping mall was definitely in order, thinking a nice piece of jewelry might be a suitable birthday present. What woman doesn't like a little bauble now and then?

As Paula started to leave the house, Pucci dutifully came scampering after her. "Be a good boy, Pucci, Mommy is going shopping for a present for Aunt Marian. I won't be long." She gave him a dog biscuit and put up the gate in the kitchen so he'd be safe. She grabbed the keys to her father's old Buick. As soon as she turned on the ignition, she was startled when the radio blasted deafeningly, full-decibel. Wow, who was in this car last, she wondered. Lowering the volume, she felt a warmth come over her, as the words of the song on the radio became clear: "You Are the Wind Beneath My Wings." This was the first time she heard this song. She felt her father's presence so strongly in the car with her; his car. Her eyes welled up with tears. Immediately, she recalled what the psychic had said. Perhaps she was being ridiculous, but whatever had just happened made her feel good. "Oh, Daddy," she said softly, wanting to acknowledge John's presence.

A few months passed and it happened again, this time at a family party. Richard and Paula drove to Staten Island to attend an engagement party for her cousin Robert's daughter. All the aunts and uncles were in attendance. As usual, at Italian parties there was way too much food—giant bowls of jumbo shrimp on ice, freshly-shucked clams, waiters passing around rumaki, chicken on skewers, baby lamb chops, and these were just the appetizers. After the main course, Italian pastries and cookies were heaped on platters on each table. Paula saw Aunt Catherine and Aunt Tessie having a cup of coffee while devouring Italian pastries, and then she noticed her Aunt Tess opening up her purse. The woman carefully wrapped up some cookies in a napkin to take home. Aunt Catherine saw Paula looking their way, and called out, "My sister thinks its all take-out!"

John's brother Ernie was dancing with his lady friend, as his two unmarried daughters looked on disapprovingly. They still didn't like the idea that their father was dating. Paula enjoyed watching the family, comfortable in the knowledge that some things were still the same.

"Richard, let's dance," she said, feeling nicely lighthearted as she dragged her husband out to the dance floor. The band was surprisingly good, playing all the standard oldies and new songs. "This is such a fun party; my father would have enjoyed it so much. I wish he were here."

"You're right about that, Paula," Richard replied, pulling her a little closer. With that, the band leader announced that the next song they would play would be the last of the evening. Standing on the dance floor, the band began to play, and the vocalist sang . . . "Wind Beneath My Wings."

"Richard, do you hear what the band is playing? He's here."

"Who's here?

"My father . . ."

Call it a coincidence, call it nonsense. But it continued. Her first Christmas without both of her parents was going to be difficult. So she decided to invite Aunt Catherine over to help boost their spirits. She knew her aunt would regale them with stories about her brothers and sisters. It would be good for the older woman, too. She didn't want her aunt to be alone this year. Catherine missed her brother terribly. "Sonofabitch," she would say repeatedly. "After your mother died, Johnny and I would say maybe we'd plan a trip together. I've never been anywhere, Paula. Or even if he just came to my house once in a while. I would have treated him like a prince. Sonofabitch," she would invariably conclude.

She agreed to come to New Jersey with the stipulation that as soon as Christmas was over, they had to drive her back to Long Island. God forbid she should be away from home for more than two or three days. The fact that several of her neighbors had Paula's telephone number really didn't matter to Paula's aunt. Richard, now the dutiful husband he had become, drove Catherine home. Paula suggested on their return trip that they stop in the city to see the tree at Rockefeller Center and perhaps stop at a few stores for the big after-Christmas sales. Richard wasn't exactly thrilled with her idea.

"Please, Hugs, just for a little while. I only want to stop at Saks Fifth Avenue and Henri Bendel."

He reluctantly agreed. "But just for an hour," he stipulated.

The city was crowded with tourists and shoppers. Paula made a mad dash into both stores, and quickly picked up some Christmas ornaments at half price. One item that caught her eye was a gold glass snow globe, the kind you pick up and shake. Inside was a figurine of the Mother Mary and the Infant Jesus. She liked it, and she quickly took the items to the register. She could see Richard was getting impatient. The next day, Paula examined her purchases to put them away for the following Christmas season. She looked at the snow globe and turned it upside down, turning the knob to play the music box. Her sister Marian had a similar snow globe that played "Joy to the World," and Paula was expecting to hear a Christmas song. It played "Wind Beneath My Wings."

Chapter 32

RECOVERY—
PHASE 2

T IME IS SUPPOSED TO HEAL ALL WOUNDS, but two
years later both sisters were still feeling the void left by
their parents. Maybe it was the damn suddenness of them
dying so soon after each other. There was no time to recover.
One day they were a happy family; the next day they were
orphans. Maybe they were too attached, they thought. Is that
possible? Being too attached to your parents? Richard once
told his wife, "Paula, you can't be daddy's little girl forever."
But that's exactly what she wanted to be. She cherished her
father's belongings, especially his army dog tags, which she
found in his jewelry case. Deciding to get them gold dipped,
she wore them around her neck on a chain. On the other
hand, Marian found comfort in her mother's collections of
recipes, cookbooks, and a pink bathrobe that her mother
had worn every day. Tangible mementos that they could feel,
touch, smell, kept them feeling close to their parents.

Rose and John were far from rich. They left no fancy
pieces of jewelry, never wore designer clothing, and left a

modest amount of cash for the girls to split between them. They once had a beautiful mahogany bedroom set, but Rose sold most of the pieces when oak furniture was all the rage. The only piece that remained was a mahogany desk, where John liked to keep his important documents. It was in this desk that the sisters found a notebook that John kept for tracking their doctor visits. Next to the name of the last doctor he'd seen, he wrote in small script, "Angel, I will be with you shortly."

They also found a letter in the desk. It was addressed to Laura, his granddaughter. He began writing it when she was just two years old, and he continued to add a paragraph every so often. Part of it read . . . "My darling Laura, I hope that I may live long enough to see you grow into a young lady, but I'm getting on in years and only God knows how many more years I have left. Anyway, what I mean and want to say is that you're a baby now, and I love you so very much. You brought great joy into my life. You may never remember me. I hope that you do. Let your mother tell you how much you enjoyed being with Papa, because I let you have your way and we enjoyed being together . . ." The letter continued about the days they played together, the walks in the park, and feeding the ducks near the pond.

When the sisters read this letter, tears rolled down their cheeks. This was their father; a man capable of great sentimentality and tenderness. Affable, well-mannered, and fervently passionate about his family, he was an extrovert, a charming jokester. No one would ever suspect how his thoughts and feelings were colored with so much heartfelt emotion. He may have looked and carried on like any Mediterranean male, but in reality he took after his beloved father, Joseph. "I'm an average guy, an immigrant's son," he would often say. Even John's pompous in-laws ultimately had to admit how they unfairly misjudged him. In fact, he became the one they sought out if they had problems to solve. If anyone needed help or a handout, he would gladly give it. "A favor, hey, if it can't get me arrested, what can I do for you?" was his rhetorical reply.

Perhaps what Paula missed most about losing him was the security and joy she felt being in his presence. Richard provided a far different love. It was romantic, supportive, analytical, cosmopolitan; the difference perhaps between Pratesi linens on one's bed and a beat-up old blanket to curl up under. Paula soon gathered that security blankets were getting scarcer.

After two years of married life and thankfully no children, JB and Nina were calling it quits. "We really got on each other's nerves, Mom. We kept fighting and making up. It wasn't getting any better. In the last few months, we've been fighting a lot more than making up. She threw my clothes out the window." This was significant, since they lived in a fourth floor apartment.

"Sure makes it easier to pack," Richard joked when Paula told him what Nina had done.

Paula thought she was over worrying about bad news, but she was wrong. Out of the blue, she got a call from Joe Day's younger brother. "Paula, I hate to call you, but this morning my parents found Joe in bed. He died in his sleep." She was dumbfounded. Joe had left his job at the Waldorf and was temporarily living at home. She figured he was taking a breather, regrouping. His brother suggested it might have been from an accidental overdose of pills and vodka. The young man who befriended her on the first day in the hotel business was dead. She was mortified. Joe was nine years younger than she was, and they were just together a few weeks ago celebrating his birthday. As she thought about this outgoing, yet not quite forthright man, she began to suspect that he was never happy with himself. He loved the disco scene and the high life of New York. Yet he never really felt comfortable in his own body and sexuality.

"Oh, Joe, I'm so sorry. I'll miss you," she said quietly to herself. It was another loss to endure.

Why did life have to be so cruel? She tried to count her blessings, but so much heartache made it difficult. Praying for relief one day, Paula had a flash of inspiration. An inner voice told her it was time to reconsider going to Italy.

When Richard again brought up the notion of taking a trip to retrace her family's heritage, she knew this was the perfect time. For reasons she couldn't quite understand, she now had a sense of urgency about it. "Richard, let's do it. I really want to go to Italy. Will you plan the trip for us? Heck, it's where my grandparents came from and where my roots are."

"Alex Haley would be honored," Richard answered gamely.

"What the heck are you talking about now?" she teased.

Excitement built with every new discussion or map Richard hauled out onto the dining table. They would talk about where they would go and what they hoped to see. Richard was a fan of popular destinations and insisted they check out places like Positano.

"Richard, don't forget Calabria. And, oh, Richard, remember Dad telling us there's even a town called Maida? Where is it? Can we go there?" Paula knew her husband was an experienced traveler. When it came to planning, organizing, and putting an itinerary together, he was superb. Perhaps that was the training he got as a marine. You could put him anywhere in the world, and he instinctively knew what road to take and how to get there. "Richard, just promise me when you plan our trip that we won't be rushing all the time. I want to relax and not be on the go twenty-four hours a day."

"Okay, if you promise me one thing in exchange," he answered, adding, "Don't pack enough to dress the whole country. Remember, my love, I'm the one who carries the bags."

When Paula told her sister about the trip, Marian didn't hesitate to say she'd take care of Pucci. "Don't worry about anything, Paula. I'll take care of the dog, the mail, and water the plants. For goodness sake, just go and enjoy yourself." Paula didn't realize this journey would put her on a path to her spiritual awakening.

Chapter 33

A JOURNEY
TO THE OLD
COUNTRY

R ICHARD PLANNED EVERY DETAIL OF THE TRIP to
ensure it would be perfect for the both of them.

"I'm not taking any chances, Paula. If I blow it, I'll never
hear the end of it from you."

He may have been right . . . that's one thing about some
stubborn Brooklyn-born Italian women, at least those born
in the 1940s and 1950s. They will cook for their men, iron
their clothing, and make mad passionate love with them, and
in return all they required were occasional displays of appre-
ciation and tenderness. And with Paula, Richard learned an
occasional piece of fine jewelry made her ecstatic.

As he outlined the trip, they would begin in Sicily's picturesque medieval town of Taormina. For the first three days
they would stay at a fifteenth century Dominican monastery
and tour the eastern coast of Sicily. From Taormina they
would travel to Messina and take a car ferry to Calabria.

Richard planned to take Paula to the town where her father's family came from near Cosenza. Once in Southern Italy, the tip of the boot, they would look for the little villages where both sets of grandparents were born. After that, they would continue to Positano, Sorrento, Pompeii, Naples—all in all, ten days in Italy and then home. Both agreed that May was the perfect time of the year to travel to Europe.

The trip from Newark to Rome started off on a high note. Being an apprehensive flyer, Paula was delighted to see that their seat assignments were 3A & 3B. The spacious leather seats even had linen cloths on which to rest their heads and wool blankets for warmth. "Ya gotta love a man who treats you right," she told Richard, sinking happily back into her first-class seat. As soon as she sat down and buckled up, the stewardess arrived.

"A glass of champagne?" she asked.

"Yes, please." Paula was going to relish every minute of this plane ride with Richard.

Their supper onboard was surprisingly good. It included a pasta dish, salad, filet mignon, and a Chianti Classico Reserve. For dessert they were served warm chocolate chip cookies and ice cream. Feeling completely relaxed, Paula rested soundly with her soft pillow and warm blanket. The short connecting flight to Fontanarossa Airport in Catania took about an hour. At the airport, the couple was greeted by a private limo driver the hotel had sent for them. The driver was a small, impeccably dressed man Paula gauged to be about sixty. "*Buon giorno*, Mr. and Mrs. Madden, welcome to Sicily. I am your driver, Gino. Please allow me to take your luggage. Our car is over there." He pointed to a shiny, black Mercedes. Paula was surprised that his English was quite good, while her Italian was almost non-existent.

"Richard, what a way to travel. I feel almost decadent."

"No kidding," he said, knowing she was in for a treat.

Gino told them that the ride to the San Domenico Palace Hotel was almost an hour. He suggested they simply relax and enjoy the view.

"*Molte grazie*, Gino," was all Paula could say. Why didn't she speak Italian, she wondered. It's such a romantic language. Then she remembered how her grandparents wanted their children and grandchildren to speak English and to really belong to their new country. In high school she took French. *Stupido*, she thought to herself.

On the drive, they discussed the history of Sicily with Gino and learned that its early immigrants came from Greece, Spain, Morocco, Norway, and many other water-bordering countries. Gino pointed out where the Mount Etna volcanic eruptions flowed to the coast near Naxos. Finally they arrived at their destination, an old monastery, converted to a hotel in 1896, and a favorite of King Edward VII, Winston Churchill, and Audrey Hepburn. It had been the Sicilian headquarters for the German high command during World War II.

The lobby had brick red tile floors laid in a herringbone pattern, high beamed ceilings, and antiques in every corner, with huge vases of fresh cut flowers everywhere. And there was a delicious scent that filled the air. Not only did the architecture date back to the Renaissance, so did the gardens—orange blossoms, roses, jasmine, lemon trees. The air was filled with their sweet scents. Richard made sure they had a luxurious junior suite, which had a private terrace with pots of colorful flowers and a stone balustrade railing that overlooked the Ionian Sea.

On the western horizon, you could see the majestic, snow-capped Mount Etna. Paula took it all in. It was the most picturesque place she had ever seen. Every element was per-fect—the blue of the sky contrasting against the turquoise sea, the fragrance of the air with the warmth of the sun kissing her shoulders. Her esthetic sense was responding to Mother Nature. How splendorous she had decorated this landscape. Paula's hands landed on her chest and, as she took a deep breath and sighed, she touched the chain and tags she was wearing. The dog tags that her Johnny had once worn. She had decided to wear them on this trip. It made her feel connected to him. If only you were here, Daddy, to see this place, she thought, if only . . .

Later that afternoon, they toured the hotel grounds and part of the town. With many remnants of the old monas-tery still intact, it was easy to go back in time. Walking in the inner courtyard with its many classical columns, Paula could readily visualize the monks dressed in their brown robes, walking along this gravel path and praying for all of humanity. The town was a shopper's paradise, with exquisite little boutiques and stylish jewelry stores along the Corso Umberto. Their first evening, they followed Gino's sugges-tion and walked into town to dine at a local restaurant for fresh fish and pasta. Since Sicilians are noted fishermen, the first course was fresh anchovies, followed by *spaghetti con le melanzane* (spaghetti with eggplant), and for the main course, grilled swordfish, delicately prepared with fresh herbs and lemon sauce. Afterward, they strolled in the palazzo where they listened to musicians playing folk songs. People filled the streets. Laughter and happiness seemed to prevail.

Taormina literally hugs the edge of the cliffs, but that evening Paula felt it was embracing her.

After three glorious days of sightseeing, Richard rented an Alfa Romeo, which they would take on the ferry at Messina to Calabria. Paula hoped for calm weather, as the waters around Messina can often develop deadly whirlpools in storms. She was reluctant to depart this heavenly island, but they had a ferry reservation and the weather was perfect to pass the Straits of Messina. The channel between Northeastern Sicily and Southern Italy (Ionian and Tyrrhenian seas) was smooth as glass that day. After parking the automobile on the transport deck, they ventured above to take in the views. The sun was shining brightly and the soft salt sea breezes blew through Paula's hair. Her eyes squinted, and she noticed another ferry passing on the right side. The name on its bow was *San Giovanni*. She took her father's patron saint's name as a good omen.

As they disembarked the ship, Richard pulled out the maps. "Keep your eyes open now, Honey Bear, and look for signs that say the Autostrada. We want A3 toward Cosenza. The highway system in Italy is very civilized, and cars can go awfully fast, so just help me and keep your eyes open." Paula commented that she was surprised to see so many highway tunnels run through huge mountains. It started as a sunny day, but after an hour's drive they were now in the shadow of a huge cloud and the rains began to pour. At one point it rained so fast and furiously that they couldn't see in front of them. Paula started to panic.

Nervously, Richard said, "Paula, I can't see a thing."

She must have said "Oh, God" a hundred times before saying, "Richard, you look straight ahead and I'll look down to see the lines on the road." They knew they couldn't stop the car and wait this out, because the cars behind them could hit them, and they really didn't want to be part of an Italian accordion. Richard drove at a snail's pace.

"Great! We finally get to Italy and we'll die on a highway," Paula yelled. Finally, they entered a long tunnel and got some relief. Paula started to breathe again. When they emerged, it was still raining but not as heavily. "Can't we get off this highway?" she pleaded.

"Pretty soon, I think the next town we'll be coming to is Maida. Let's stop there and grab some lunch," Richard suggested. The rain finally subsided and the sun began to shine once again.

The three major provinces of Calabria are Reggio de Calabria in the south, Catanzaro in the middle bordered by both the Ionian and Tyrrhenian seas, and Cosenza in the north bordering on Basilicata. Just off the main road in Catanzaro lies the small town of Maida. They just had to visit it. After all, it was the family name. Richard informed Paula that this remote Calabrian village became famous in 1806, when the British Army under Sir General John Stuart handed Napoleon's armies their first defeat ever, which eventually turned the tides in favor of the British at Waterloo. The elated Brits named a prosperous section of London Maida Vale in honor of their victory at the Battle of Maida in Italy. Paula recalled that her father once told her that he had visited there when he was stationed in England.

The small, hilly town of Maida is far from a tourist destination. When they arrived, they saw little to distinguish it, other than its name. It was a quiet Sunday afternoon, and wherever the locals were, they certainly weren't out and about. There was something lazy, even lethargic about the place. After the morning they had, crossing the Straits and fighting the weather changes, they were ravenous. There was no restaurant in sight, so they parked the car and decided to see what they could find on foot. A few teenage boys passed by, and Paula asked them where the nearest restaurant was. They directed them to go up the road, where they came upon a quaint ristorante called Nausicaa. The interior was plain with several rectangular tables topped with white linen cloths, the ceiling rustic with exposed wood beams, and an orange stone floor. It looked clean, and that's all that mattered to Paula.

The proprietor was most cordial, *"Parla Inglese?"* Paula asked.

"No," was his reply. She then spotted what looked like his entire family eating their Sunday dinner in the back room. This might explain why the town was so quiet; everyone was at home enjoying supper together. It brought back fond memories of her childhood and Sunday afternoon dinners with all the relatives, at which they sat for hours eating one course after another.

The proprietor sat them next to a table of two older gentlemen, who were dining and drinking contentedly. Paula pointed to what they had just been served and said, "Due per *favore et due vino rosso, grazie.*" The owner brought them fresh bread and olive oil. After a while, he came out of the kitchen with big bowls of homemade pappardelle with wild mushrooms. Savoring every morsel, Paula was trying to detect the subtle flavors. The thick, rich brown sauce, sweet onions, and thinly cut woodsy mushrooms were all topped off with some freshly grated cheese. The pasta was cooked to perfection—al dente. Was that Marsala wine she tasted in this, as well? Their ravenous hunger had been satiated with this hearty peasant meal.

Thanking the proprietor, Richard tipped him generously. In return, he gave them a bottle of red table wine for their journey. The label read "Vino da Tavola, Ristorante Nausicaa, bottled in Maida." Wouldn't it be wonderful if she could show this bottle to her father, was what registered in Paula's thoughts. They left contented, refreshed, and ready to continue their trip.

Paula was pleased that they only stayed one night in Cosenza. The hotel room was a far cry from the one they had just left in Taormina. The Executive Hotel on Via Marconi in Rende was a modern business hotel on a busy road adjacent to an industrial area with lots of truck traffic. After check-in, they followed the map across Cosenza toward Donnici Superiore, the town where her grandfather was born. The late Sunday afternoon traffic was heavy as they departed the city and moved up the hills in the little rented Alfa Romeo. As they drove, Paula could see the fertile land, its grape vineyards and olive trees. This was where her grandfather was taught the art of winemaking. These sunny hillside towns produce the wines of Italy; the distinctness of the soil imparting its flavor and richness into the soul of the grape. Every section of Italy produces its own little liquid gold—Barolo, Santa Maddalena, Soave, Frascati, Bardolino, Valpolicella, Montepulciano, Chianti—all wines that had been on her parents' dining room table at one time or another. Richard discovered that there were more than twenty regions that produce wines in Italy. Knowing her husband, Paula knew that he would delight in sampling all of them.

They were now approaching the town where her grandfather was born. Both of them felt a bubbling excitement. They were finally there. To her delight and surprise the streets were filled with people. What's going on, she thought. "Please,

Richard, let's park the car and walk around." She wanted to experience it all, as she knew this town was off the tourist route.

A local policeman was directing traffic, and in her poor Italian she asked, "*Che cosa e'?*" He told her it was the feast of Saint Michael the Archangel. They were able to catch the tail end of the procession, and watched the men of the town carry a life-size statue of the saint. After an hour of walking, they decided to call it a day, and head back to the hotel. Paula was pleased that she was able to visit her grandfather's hometown that afternoon. It was just fifty miles south from her grandmother's town of Tarsia. She found it ironic that two young people, both raised in the province of Cosenza, never met until they came to America. Isn't it strange how fate connects people? Little did she realize that fate would soon connect her in a way that she could never imagine.

Chapter 34

THE GIFT

PAULA WASN'T SURE WHY, but as she packed for their trip to Italy, she gathered some of the old documents that included her grandparents' birth and marriage certificates and two yellowing black and white photographs that her grandmother had kept in her wallet. She hadn't a clue to who these people in the photographs were, but her intuition said to pack them.

Both Paula and Richard were excited about proceeding to Tarsia, the birthplace of her paternal grandmother.

"Angelina, we're on our way!" Richard said. His spirits were as high as the gear on the little Alfa Romeo as it picked up speed slowly. Just over an hour later, they arrived and were not disappointed at their first impression. Tarsia is a little fortress town perched on a hilltop with a population of a few thousand people. It sits several hundred feet above the flatlands of the Lago di Tarsia, beside which the town's cemetery is situated. As they drove past it, they surmised that most of Grandma's deceased relatives must be buried there.

Continuing up into the hills, they got to the village square with their car bumpity-bumping over its cobblestone streets. Richard noticed a church, but he kept driving. They didn't get far. The width of the street kept getting narrower and narrower. The Alfa was small to begin with, but now its side mirrors were inches away from hitting the buildings.

"Richard, this is ridiculous. We can't keep going. Back up the car, and let's stop at that church," Paula suggested.

He shifted gears and deftly headed backward, parking across from the church. Their legs were stiff and needed a good stretch. They got out of the car and happily rotated their upper bodies. Being a tall guy crammed into a tiny vehicle didn't help Richard's aching back. Within minutes of looking at the church, Richard uttered in surprise, "Paula, look at the name of this church—Chiesa Di S. Maria Del Seggio. From your documents, I think this is where your grandmother was baptized." They checked the papers in her purse, and he was right, as usual. Paula didn't remember that name, but Richard had the ability to remember everything, so why should this surprise her now? The building had hand-carved wooden doors, with a massive iron cross on top of its archway that faced the lower hills. She stared and stared at it, then said "Bear, I'd like to stay here a while. Would you try to find a shop and get us some bottled water for the ride back?"

Paula was in total amazement that they had found this church without even looking for it. She just wanted to linger and absorb this site and space. She gently whispered, "Daddy, can you believe this, can you believe I'm standing in front of the church where your mother was baptized?"

She was deep in thought when an old man came up to her. She couldn't imagine what he wanted. Mostly, he just seemed curious about her. In her barely passable Italian, she spouted her routine greeting, *"Buon giorno, senor. Parla Inglese?"*

"*No Inglese. Parlo Italiano,*" he answered. So much for that. Now she took out the writing pad and pencil she kept for just such situations.

She handed them to him, and said, "*Lo scriva, per favore.*" ("Write it down, please.") He merely looked puzzled. They weren't making much progress, but throughout their encounter, Paula had noticed a dark-haired woman standing on a second floor balcony across the street. She kept looking in Paula's direction, and before she realized it, the woman was on the street approaching her. For some reason when the old man saw her coming their way, he quietly walked off.

The woman appeared to be in her sixties and stood about five feet tall. She wore a black dress with a geometric, colored print design and a small gold chain around her neck. Wavy, short brown hair framed her oval-shaped face. She walked right up to Paula and started speaking rapid-fire Italian. "*Non parlo Italiano, signora,*" was all Paula could get out.

"*Aspetti, uno minuto,*" Paula said, as she remembered the photos she was carrying. Fumbling in her purse, she finally found them in a side compartment, where she had put them for safekeeping. Pointing to the photos, Paula uttered in her half-assed half-Italian, half-English, "My *famiglia* is from here . . . *mi nonna* is from Tarsia." Smiling and now even more animated than before, the woman started to wave her hands up and down, gesturing to Paula to come with her.

By this time, a young woman in her early twenties joined them. Paula was relieved to hear her speak a little English. The older woman repeated to her in Italian, "*La famiglia.*"

At that moment, Richard came back with several bottles of water. "Hey, what's going on here? I leave for five minutes and you have a crowd."

"Richard, this lady had been looking at me from her balcony across the street. For some reason, she came down and started talking to me."

Paula then turned to the younger woman, asking, "Please, can you tell me what she is saying?"

"My aunt wants you to come upstairs to her house. It's important, she says. Please, will you go with her?"

"Why?" Paula asked.

"These photos are her family," she replied.

"No, you're mistaken. My grandmother was born in this town. These are pictures of my family." A mystified Paula turned to Richard. "What should we do?"

"Let's go up and see," he responded, and agreed to follow the two women. Richard locked the car, taking his camera with him. The house was three stories high, situated on the side of a reinforced cliff. There was an open space on the ground floor with apartments on the second and third, all constructed with the same pale-colored stone as the church that stood less than a hundred feet away. The niece asked them to take a seat on the sofa.

"My name is Ida, and my aunt's name is Antoinetta," she said. An older man walked into the room. She introduced him. "This is my uncle, my aunt's husband Damiano Marino." He was downstairs, and hearing the commotion, he had decided to see what was going on upstairs. "Please, sit. My aunt wants to show you something," Ida requested.

Antoinetta went into another room. A few minutes later, she returned, carrying a large black and white photograph. All smiles, she held it up for her guests to see. Paula's mind couldn't comprehend what the picture was doing in this house.

"That's my grandmother!" Paula half-shouted in disbelief. "Richard, why would she have a picture of my grandmother?"

"*Aspetta*," Antoinetta said, motioning them to wait. She went back into the room and emerged with more photographs. The next one she held up was of Ernie Maida, Paula's uncle. Then she held up another picture—a young man attired in an American army uniform from World War II. "Oh my God, that's my father, my Johnny!" Paula cried.

Paula heard Ida saying, "*Quello è il suo padre. . . Giovanni è suo padre!*" Tears of joy were streaming down Paula's face.

Neither Paula nor Richard could explain what had just happened. By accident, they had come across relatives. Quite by happenstance—or was it? They stopped at a place where they had never been before, and now they were standing in a relative's living room.

Paula couldn't stop crying, her heart was pounding. Richard gave his wife his handkerchief. Ida brought them a glass of red wine. Finally, after Paula composed herself, she learned the details.

Antoinetta's mother and Paula's grandmother were sisters. This woman who came to meet Paula on the street was her grandmother's niece, her father's first cousin. Maria Francesca, Antoinetta's mother, was the sole sibling who remained in Tarsia to take care of her aging parents and the family's olive groves. She was the sister who was left behind. She married Luigi Rimola and had seven daughters and two sons. The Rimola family owned 300 hectares of Tarsia's olive and orange groves, or that was what Paula thought she heard in her excitement. After gathering her composure, she went over to the window; they opened the shutters so Paula could get a view of the countryside. The hot afternoon sun poured into the room as Paula adjusted her eyes, and then she saw the verdant land. As far as the eye could see, acres and acres were filled with orange and olive trees. Ida pointed to a stone house located to the right of the property that sat on an angle beneath them. "That is the house your grandmother was born in," she told Paula.

Paula stood there motionless, an incredulous stare upon her face. She looked at Richard for some reassurance that she wasn't imagining or dreaming all of this. But by this time, there was lots of activity around them.

"What's going on?" Paula asked Ida.

"My aunt is calling her sisters and the rest of our family to come here and meet you." "You mean there are more relatives?"

"Of course! Her sisters Menuccia and Lina are coming over now." As it turned out, one of the two photos that Paula had brought with her included these three sisters, her grandmother's nieces.

"But I assumed all the relatives left in Italy were dead," Paula blurted out.

"No," she smiled, "we are still living!"

The rest of that afternoon was filled with relatives coming and going. Antoinetta insisted they stay for a dinner. Although it was a Monday, she prepared a traditional Sunday meal more quickly than one can say *"pasta e fagioli."* Less than four hours after wondering what they would find in Tarsia, Paula was dining with relatives. No one stopped talking at the table. That in itself was a giveaway that, yes, this had to be her family.

Richard took lots of pictures that day, so they could remember this astonishing afternoon and share them with Marian back home. It was getting late and dusk would soon be upon them, and they knew they had to depart shortly.

They exchanged addresses and phone numbers, along with innumerable kisses and hugs. Antoinetta gave her newly found cousin some cheese, prosciutto, figs, and a bottle of Damiano's homemade wine to take with them on their journey, just in case they got hungry or thirsty. Ah yes, another family trait.

Before they left, Menuccia gave Richard a bottle of aftershave. He had the impression she might have saved it for a hoped-for beau. In any event, it was something that was special to her. She was surprisingly tall and slim, animated, quick to laugh, and clearly bright. He learned that she was the principal of Tarsia's only school and that her sister Lina was one of the teachers. The students were in good hands, of that he was sure.

Their gestures were so genuine, Paula wanted to reciprocate. She gave her cousin Antoinetta the earrings she was wearing, gold-plated dangling pierced earrings with a faux diamond in the center. She didn't mention that they were not real; she assumed the woman would know. And for Menuccia, she took off the cream and pale green silk scarf she was wearing around her neck, and handed it to her. More kisses, more hugs ensued. "*Grazie!* Thank you! Don't be a stranger! Come back! Come see us in America!"

About an hour after they had started to leave, they finally left. Richard noted to Paula, another family trait, long goodbyes. They still had a four-hour drive to Positano ahead of them, but Paula was riding high. She was euphoric reflecting on the events of the day. "Richard, can you believe it?" she chirped repeatedly. "It's unbelievable!"

Paula knew with certainty this day had changed her life. It lifted her up from the despair over first losing her mother, then her Johnny. No matter how she tried to analyze what happened, it was inconceivable that the events of the day were mere coincidences. Of all places, why did they stop there? And, why, at the very time she stood outside the church, would her cousin be on her balcony and notice her? In fact, she had asked Ida, "Why did your aunt come down to talk to me?"

Ida replied, "When my aunt saw your face, you looked familiar to her. She felt as if she knew you. But not your husband, just you."

During the rest of their journey, Paula's state of mind was exhilarated, and physically she felt infused with energy. Positano by the sea was a scenic wonderland with narrow streets and alleyways with abundant shops that led down to the stony beaches. But nothing would ever compare to that glorious spring day in Tarsia. There was no doubt in her mind that her father's hand had guided her along this journey. At last, her grief was erased and replaced with peace. The epiphany and meaning of what happened that day suddenly became clear.

Paula intuitively knew that her father had transmitted a message in a way that was so like him—through his love of family. Every nuance, every gesture and sequence of events was as it should have been. Nothing was coincidental. With unflinching clarity, Paula knew when it was her time to depart the tangible world to enter the celestial one, her Johnny, the loving father that he was, would come to take her home.

End

PHOTOGRAPHS

John Maida in his army uniform off to war.

Johnny playing with Paula

A family of three—John, Rose, and Paula

John and Rose Maida attending a formal wedding in NYC.

The old photo Paula carried with her to Italy of three unknown women. She found out they were her cousins, and all still living!

While Paula stands in front of the church in Tarsia, a man approaches her.

A woman comes down from her balcony to talk to Paula, and her niece then joins them.

In the home of her newly found cousin, Antoinetta shows Paula photographs and documents relating to her father and family.

Cousins . . . do you see the family resemblance?

All hugs and smiles from cousin Menuccia.

Lina (Menuccia's sister), Paula, and Menuccia

RECIPES

My Father's Meatballs

Every Wednesday and Sunday we ate some form of pasta and meatballs. It was a ritual . . . and so delicious. Mangia!

Ingredients:

- 1 lb. ground chuck
- 1 slice good white bread (remove crust)
- 1/3 cup milk at room temperature
- 2 tablespoons finely chopped onion
- 2 cloves finely chopped garlic
- 2 heaping tablespoons of finely chopped parsley
- Freshly ground pepper (salt optional)
- 1/3 cup grated Pecorino Romano cheese
- 1 egg (lightly beaten)
- Oil to fry (either canola or olive)
- Dad's secret ingredient, 1 tablespoon Heinz ketchup

Mix Ingredients As Follows:

In a mixing bowl, break up the ground meat in pieces with your hands; put the slice of white bread in the milk, and mash with a fork. Add torn pieces of the wet bread and milk mush to the chopped meat.

Beat the egg separately; add to the mixture.

Add the remaining above ingredients and mix thoroughly by hand.

Put a small amount of the meat mixture into the palm of your hand and using both hands form a medium-size meatball. Put the meatballs on a tray to rest about 15 minutes. You can use this time to clean up.

In a frying pan pour enough oil to cover the bottom of the pan (about 1/4 inch deep).

Heat the oil until it's very hot and then reduce to medium-high heat. Gently slide the meatballs into the pan with a large spoon—carefully, so you don't break the mixture. Fry the meatballs until golden brown on all sides (turn with a spoon). Don't rush this step.

Remove each meatball as it is cooked. Place on plate lined with paper towels to absorb excess oil. Serve them as is— or add them to a tomato sauce (gravy), and simmer for 30 minutes.

An optional cooking method is to place meatballs on a well-oiled cookie sheet and bake at 350 degrees for 30 minutes. Then add to sauce and simmer.

Makes about 10/12 meatballs depending on size (you can double this recipe and freeze after they are cooked). Note: Some people like to add raisins or pignoli nuts to their meatballs (I like raisins).

ROSE'S STRUFFOLI
(HONEY CLUSTERS)

Mom would make this dessert a few days before Christmas
Eve. Now Marian makes it and triples the recipe. Struffoli
are tiny balls, deep fried and honey coated and arranged in
a cone shape. It wouldn't be Christmas Eve without them!

Ingredients:

- 2 cups pre-sifted flour

- 1/4 teaspoon salt

- 3 eggs

- 1/2 teaspoon vanilla

- 1 cup of Golden Blossom honey, plus one tablespoon
  sugar

- Sprinklers—tiny multicolored candies

- Oil for deep frying—canola or vegetable oil

Mix Ingredients As Follows:

Heat oil to 365 degrees in a deep pot or an automatic deep
fryer.

Meanwhile in a large bowl add the flour and salt. Make a
well in the center of the flour. Add one egg at a time, mixing
slightly after each egg is added. Add vanilla.

Mix well to make a soft dough. Turn dough onto a lightly floured surface and knead. Knead again. Divide dough in half.

Lightly roll each half about 1/4" thick to form a rectangle. Cut dough with a pastry cutter or knife into strips of 1/4" wide. Using the palm of your hand, roll strips to pencil thickness. Cut into pieces about 1/2" long and form into tiny balls.

When the oil is hot, drop in and fry only as many pieces of dough as will float on top; do not crowd. One layer deep is adequate. Fry three to five minutes until golden brown, turning occasionally. Using a slotted spoon, remove the tiny balls from the fat, and throw into a brown paper bag (to absorb the oil).

Meanwhile, on top of the stove in another pan over low heat, pour one cup of honey, plus the sugar. Stir until thin. Remove from the heat and add the fried balls. Stir constantly until all pieces are coated with the honey/sugar mixture. Let cool for ten minutes (either outside or someplace cool inside). You just want to chill slightly so you can put them on a pretty dessert dish and form into a cone shape. Sprinkle with the multicolored candies, wrap with wax paper and foil. Store in a cool, dry place until ready to serve.

My mother usually hid the struffoli in the basement until Christmas Eve. If she didn't, we would be picking on them, and she would have to make more. This recipe serves about eight people.

CHRISTMAS EVE SCUNGILLI SALAD

The men in my family inhale this dish. Two days before Christmas Eve I prepare this dish, usually doubling this recipe. Scungilli is conch. I now use sliced, canned scungilli, which saves a ton of time rather then fresh or frozen (which is sometimes hard to find). If some of the sliced scungilli pieces are too big, just cut into smaller pieces.

Ingredients:

- 2 large cans sliced scungilli, drained (I use La Monica brand, 29 oz. cans)
- Garlic—3 large cloves finely chopped or more to taste
- Olive oil—1/2 cup good quality extra virgin olive oil
- Salad olives with pimentos, drained—1 cup chopped, 8 oz.
- Black pitted olives sliced, drained—small can about 4 oz.
- Lemon juice—1/2 cup freshly squeezed, no pits, please
- Celery—1 full cup chopped celery—peel stalks first
- Parsley—1/2 cup fresh Italian flat parsley, chopped fine
- Oregano—1/2 teaspoon dried
- Celery salt—1/2 teaspoon
- Pepper—freshly ground pepper to taste

- Salt—if needed, use sea salt only
- Vinegar peppers/hot peppers in a jar—this is optional, use if you like a little heat.

Mix Ingredients As Follows:

Open cans of scungilli and drain very well in a colander.

Put in a large bowl and add the above ingredients

Using a large spoon, mix well. Cover and let stand overnight or two in the refrigerator so the flavors get to open up.

I usually serve this on a large fish platter that has been covered with red leaf lettuce. Spoon the scungilli salad on top. When ready to serve, drizzle some olive oil on top. Serve with fresh lemon wedges.

Serves six people

SCROD PUTTANESCA

Neapolitans love tomatoes and simple fish dishes. This dish is tasty, satisfying, and easy to prepare.

I usually serve it as a main course in soup bowls with hot, crusty Italian bread (dip the bread into the sauce) and a green salad. Serves two hearty eaters.

Ingredients:

- 1 lb. fresh scrod or cod—get a nice thick piece
- 1/4 cup olive oil (plus one tablespoon for top of fish)
- 2 cloves garlic—finely chopped
- 1 medium onion—sliced
- 1 can diced tomatoes (about ¾ cup—drain juices)
- 1 small can sliced black olives—drain
- 2 or 3 fresh basil leaves—chopped
- 3 teaspoons capers—drained
- celery salt
- salt & pepper (use sea salt)
- Hot pepper flakes (optional)
- Parsley to garnish—flat Italian and not curly parsley

Mix Ingredients As Follows:

Preheat oven to 350 degrees. In a sauté pan, add olive oil, garlic, and onion. Cook on low heat five to ten minutes until onion is transparent. Add canned tomatoes, black olives, capers, salt and pepper, and simmer for a few minutes.

Put fish in a lightly oiled Pyrex baking dish (skin side down). Sprinkle with celery salt. Pour tomato mixture on top and drizzle more oil on top.

Bake 15/20 minutes until fish flakes with a fork. Oven temperatures vary, so check the fish. Do not overcook.

Serve in soup bowls with juices; garnish with chopped parsley.

For dessert I usually serve Sfogliatelle (sweet ricotta turnover), which can be purchased from your local Italian bakery.

LINGUINE WITH
WHITE CLAM SAUCE

This dish is so easy to prepare. Most people complicate the recipe and add too many ingredients. Just taste the sauce and check if it needs more sea salt or herbs.

Always use fresh clams and lots of parsley. This serves two hearty eaters as a main course, or four as a first course.

Ingredients:

- 1 lb. good Italian linguine pasta (I like Barilla brand pasta)
- 2 dozen Little Neck Clams (small hard-shelled clams) scrubbed. I do not use any other type of clams. Little Necks have the best flavor for this dish, in my opinion.
- Flat Italian parsley, chopped 1/2 cup or more to taste (I like loads of parsley)
- Clam juice, two bottles (shake the bottles)
- Oregano—1/4 teaspoon dried
- Celery salt—1/2 teaspoon
- 2/3 cup good Italian oil (enough oil to cover bottom of the pan)
- 5 cloves garlic (or to taste) cut in slivers
- Salt & pepper (use sea salt when preparing fish dishes)

Mix Ingredients As Follows:

To begin with, wash and scrub the clams using a small brush. Put them in a bowl of cold water, add one tablespoon sea salt. Put in refrigerator until ready to use.

Prepare to boil your water for the pasta in a big pot.

In a deep pan or Dutch oven type pan, add the olive oil and garlic. Sauté until lightly golden; do not burn. Add the clam juice, parsley, oregano, celery salt, pepper, and simmer for five/ten minutes.

When the pasta water comes to a boil, you can add the fresh clams to the sauce to steam open (cover the pan). Put on low/medium flame.

Throw the pasta in the boiling water, which has been salted, stirring occasionally, and cook until al dente.

Drain pasta and add the sauce and fresh clams. Do not eat any clams that have not opened. Garnish the top with fresh chopped parsley. True Italians do not use grated cheese on fish dishes.

Fresh-Tasting Tomato Sauce

In the old country, cooks would probably use fresh red plum tomatoes kissed by the Mediterranean sun to make a great tasting sauce. Today, many cooks under utilize canned tomato paste which has an intense rich flavor of fresh tomatoes. These ingredients can be kept on your pantry shelf, and make a quick and easy sauce to prepare to accompany just about anything.

Ingredients:

- 2 large cans Italian peeled tomatoes in their juices (I prefer San Marzano – 28 oz. can)
- 1 small can Italian tomato paste (6 oz. can)
- 5/6 tablespoons good Italian olive oil or more (lightly cover the bottom of the sauce pan)
- Four sprigs fresh basil (or dried if fresh not available)
- 1/4 teaspoon celery salt
- 1/4 teaspoon dried oregano
- Garlic, depending on the size – three or four cloves (to taste)
- 1/4 cup liquid, either water or red wine (I usually open up a bottle of my favorite house wine, "Old Vine Red" by Marietta Cellars)
- Salt and pepper to taste

Mix Ingredients As Follows:

In a deep pot, sauté garlic in olive oil. Add the small can of tomato paste, stir and simmer a few minutes. Open the two cans of peeled tomatoes and pour in large bowl. With clean hands, squeeze the tomatoes so that they are crushed and not so chunky. Add the two cans of peeled tomatoes and their juices to the pot. Use either a little water or wine to clean out the empty tomato cans, add this liquid to the sauce pot. Add remaining dry ingredients.

Let the sauce slowly simmer for thirty-five minutes, and taste occasionally to see if it needs more salt/pepper or oregano.

You can use this sauce over pasta, meatballs or sausage. Don't forget to sprinkle Parmesan cheese on everything (with the exception of fish). Enough sauce to serve six people over pasta.

Acknowledgments

M Y FIRST THANK YOU goes to a very special lady, my cousin, Andrea Giambrone. She was my sounding board and encouraged me to follow my dream; give birth to "Meatballs." There is no way I could have written this book without her help.

Andrea has lived most of her adult life in an area she describes as "approximately a million dollars south of Beverly Hills." She is a successful advertising writer who heads up her own company; a columnist and guest lecturer at events where a healthy attitude and a good dose of laughter are on the menu (it is her voice that you hear in the dialogue of our sassy diminutive aunts).

To my beloved parents, Rose and John . . . thank you for your extraordinary parenting skills. Mom, you had class and style, and nourished your family with love and food. "My Johnny" . . . your joy, enthusiasm, humor and devotion will be with me always. Marian, you will always be baby sister to me - I can't imagine my life without you. To my loving son, JB, for all that we've been through together you continue to amaze me. You are living the life you desired with a loving wife by your side in Southern California; started a new business venture, and continue to compose and write music (aka Jonathan Christian). And to my niece, Laura, you brought bliss to your grandfather in his later years, and now I am the recipient of your light.

We all need a team of girlfriends to guide us when times are difficult, give honest feedback, offer expertise when needed, and celebrate life together. My team consists of the fabulous five: Phyllis Caruana, Joanne McQuigg, Linda Postell, Karen Topjian, and Linda Yanakas. These uber-ladies and caring friends help me make sense of what is going on in my life. I have learned so much from each of you—thank you.

How can you publish a book without professional assistance? It's almost impossible. Cheers to Mark Bergeron and Peter Chamberlain of Publishers' Design and Production Services in Massachusetts for their patience with this neophyte author.

And finally, my husband, and unwavering supporter, Richard Madden; knowing that you wanted me to succeed, and helping me pull this together speaks volumes. I thank you from my heart. As my Mother so often said, "It's not how you start up in life that matters, but how you end up."

♥

About the Author

Paula Maida Mooney is proud to tell people that she grew up in Brooklyn, New York, or as some of her colorful relatives pronounced it, Brook-a-lini.

Professionally, Paula has had a career as an interior designer and antique appraiser. For the past several years, she has been fortunate to pursue her other interests—promoting non-profit organizations in her community. She is active on several boards and enjoys her association with a local access television station, where she can be seen behind and in front of the camera. Another organization dear to her heart is a dog rescue group. When time permits, she enjoys being a foster mom to homeless pups.

Authors Note: If you wish to have Paula discuss her memoir at your book club, she can be contacted at: myfatherslastmeatballs@gmail.com